WORSHIPPING TOGETHER

Worshipping Together

Published on behalf of
THE PANEL ON WORSHIP
of The Church of Scotland
by THE SAINT ANDREW PRESS,
121 George Street, Edinburgh EH2 4YN

First published in 1991 by THE SAINT ANDREW PRESS on behalf of
THE PANEL ON WORSHIP
121 George Street, Edinburgh EH2 4YN

ISBN 0 86153 128 0

British Library Cataloguing in Publication Data
Worshipping together.
          1. Church of Scotland. Public Worship - Rites
          264.05233

          ISBN 0-86153-128-0

This book has been set in 12/14 pt Times Roman.

Printed and Bound by Bell and Bain Ltd., Glasgow

Contents

Introduction

I AM delighted to introduce and commend this publication to the Church, not least because it reflects the conviction that worship involves the whole people of God.

Though in a sense this is essentially a recovery of what worship should always be, there have been clear signs in recent years of greater participation by congregations. And the fuller involvement of elders can be seen as part of this welcome trend.

The conduct of worship by Kirk Session Teams lies largely in the future, and in preparing this material the Panel on Worship has had to envisage what kind of help would be most valuable. We hope it will prove useful to have both guidelines on planning and order and also several full sets of prayers. Depending on the circumstances, elders may wish to follow the sample prayers closely or adapt them freely.

We are conscious that elders have no formal training in worship and that this booklet can provide only basic guidance and resources. However elders need not feel ill-equipped for the task. They bring to it, not theological training, but their own valid experience of being the Church in the world. Our hope and prayer is that, within the framework of Church of Scotland services, elders will bring their own insights to illumine God's Word and help to make worship and life one.

ANDREW SCOBIE
Convener, Panel on Worship

Note

THIS BOOK is designed to be used both in preparing a service and at the service itself. Especially in an emergency, there would be nothing amiss in taking it into the church and reading it verbatim at the appropriate points in the service. It is hoped that the layout and the size of the print will prove convenient for such occasions.

The provision of blank pages is seen as an essential part of the book. They should become a register of such things as the occasion and date of service; the Praise Lists, Prayers, and Readings used; and the names of the people who took part. They could also be used for the recording of prayers composed by individuals or the group, and for noting the titles of books, tapes, and videos that have been found helpful both in preparation and at the service.

It is hoped that the book, with its local additions, will become a valuable congregational resource for worship. The Panel on Worship would always be grateful to hear from any congregation about any particular experience of worship that might be of interest to the wider Church.

CHARLES ROBERTSON
Honarary Secretary, Panel on Worship

Guidelines

THERE ARE varying circumstances in which elders might be responsible for the conduct of public worship.

There may be an emergency due to the indisposition of a minister, as acknowledged in the most recent General Assembly legislation regulating the conduct of public worship, Act II 1986; and at very short notice an elder might have to 'step into the breach'. With increasing numbers of linked charges there is the possibility of elders conducting services in one part of a linkage in accordance with arrangements made by the Presbytery. And the General Assembly of 1988 confirmed that the provisions of the Act would permit, again with Presbytery approval, the conduct of worship by Kirk Session teams, that is by a group of elders sharing responsibility and acting together.

This material is offered to help in these, and other, circumstances.

1 PLANNING

The conduct of worship by elders should always take place under the guidance of a supervising minister—the Parish Minister or Interim Moderator—and elders should consult with the minister wherever possible. This is particularly important when a sermon is being preached.

Whether a service is being conducted by a minister or by elders, careful planning is always necessary. If a team is involved, thought needs to be given to the whole service and agreement reached on the various duties and on the involvement of those who are to take part. There should always be

1

consultation with the organist or leader of praise, and, where children attend part of the service before going to Sunday School, with the Sunday School staff.

Nearer the time of the service those taking part should have opportunity to rehearse. People need to discover the right pace and pitch for speaking in a large building, allowing time for the voice to travel, and ensuring that they are heard. This is even more important if there is a sound amplification system. Care should be taken to avoid awkward mannerisms; for example men should not jangle money in their pockets! Where a group of elders is involved, it should be arranged where each person is to sit and when each person is to move to the lectern or the pulpit. It is probably better that the whole group does not sit in the front facing the congregation, but that the person mainly responsible should perhaps remain in front of the congregation during the service, while others come forward as required.

2   THEME

When the group meets to consider the content of the service, the planning should begin with the choice of Bible readings. Readings should determine the theme: do not choose a theme and then look for readings which fit it. The lessons may be read by elders, or by members of the congregation. It is desirable and helpful for the readings to be taken from a lectionary, that is, from a list of readings for each Sunday in the calendar of the Christian Year. This allows the worship of an individual congregation to be part of the worship of the whole Church, and it also ensures that over a period of time the main subjects of the Bible are represented.

The lectionary most widely used in the Church of Scotland is that printed in *The Book of Common Order* which covers a two year period. A copy of this lectionary is included at section 7. A simple calculation can determine the place of a particular Sunday in the calendar; indeed most diaries provide this information. For the purpose of this lectionary, the year begins on the 9th Sunday before Christmas. This is also when the change is made from First Year to Second Year. In 1990, the lectionary moves from Second Year to First Year, and alternates thereafter annually on the 9th Sunday before Christmas. The four Sundays in Advent are counted before Christmas, the six Sundays in Lent before Easter. The Sundays after Easter lead to Ascension, Pentecost and then to a large section of the calendar of Sundays counted after Pentecost.

3   ORDER

Within the tradition of the Church of Scotland generally, certain elements are recognised as being normal in a service. Local circumstances may require adaptation, but there are outlines provided in *The Book of Common Order*, and these should serve as a guide. The service consists of three sections:

   (i)   *Approach to God*
        An invitation to worship
        Hymn, or Psalm
        Call to prayer (often in words of Scripture)
        Prayer
        Hymn

   (ii)   *The Word of God*
        Old Testament reading
        Psalm (sung, or said responsively)
        New Testament readings: Epistle
                               Gospel
        Hymn
        Proclamation of the Word

   (iii)   *Response to the Word of God*
        (The Apostles' Creed)

Offerings
Prayers and Lord's Prayer
Intimations
Hymn
Benediction

The *Church Hymnary: Third Edition (CH3)* is arranged in this same order, and in most cases hymns for each part of the service will be chosen from the appropriate section of the hymn book.

4   CHILDREN

While there is a trend towards the inclusion of children in the whole service, it remains the practice in many congregations for children to attend the first part of the service and then to leave for Sunday School. Often there is a short address for the children while they are in church and it may be convenient for this to follow the first prayer. It is desirable that the address be given by someone who is used to speaking with children; for example, a Sunday School Leader could provide an introduction to the subject of the main Sunday School lesson, thus informing the adult congregation of the theme of the Sunday School teaching. Alternatively, it can be linked to the Bible readings for the day, thus introducing the children to the main theme of the service in Church.

5   PRAYERS

Examples for the prayers are given in the services which follow. The first prayer, which may be introduced by Scripture verses, normally consists of approach to God, prayer for forgiveness, and petition. A promise or assurance of forgiveness for those who are penitent, normally in biblical form, may be included. Either at this point, or in the prayer of dedication later in the service, the Collect of the day can be included. These collects, linking with the themes of the Christian Year, are printed in *The Book of Common Order* and are also included in section 7. The second main prayer, usually containing thanksgiving, prayers for others, dedication, commemoration of the faithful departed and the Lord's Prayer, forms part of the response to the word of God. It may be appropriate that the people should participate in this prayer, perhaps in the form of a simple response. For this prayer also examples are offered, though the needs of the time will suggest relevant topics. Prayer for the work of the Church should be included (for which guidance is given in the Prayer Calendar and the linked sections in *Life and Work*) and for particular needs both of the wider world and the local community.

Those leading worship are offering prayer on behalf of the congregation: prayers should therefore be relatively short, clearly spoken, unhurried, and perhaps include pauses or short times of silence to allow the congregation to make the prayer their own.

6   HYMNS AND PSALMS

Singing is one of the most important ways in which the people participate in worship in corporate acts of praise. But hymns may also express the other elements of worship and should be chosen to fit the various parts of the service. Here the arrangement of the hymns in the *Church Hymnary: Third Edition (CH3)* in the sequence of the service is particularly helpful. Hymns should be chosen to relate to the theme of the readings or to known needs of the congregation. Normally the actual choice of hymns should involve consultation with the organist.

Section 5 offers suggestions for a service for each Sunday in two years. It is based on *The Year's Praise*, published by The Saint Andrew Press for the Panel on Worship and includes an item for each Sunday from the supplement to *CH3, Songs of God's People*. To encourage a wider use of Psalms, *The Year's Psalms* is set out in section 6.

7   PROCLAMATION OF THE WORD

Normally, where a sermon is to be preached, there will be consultation between the person responsible and the minister of the charge or the interim moderator.

The sermon is perhaps a part of the service which Kirk Session Teams may feel least qualified to tackle. However, it can be quite short, and not so daunting a task as a longer talk. Where possible a commentary on the Bible passage should be consulted. Where library facilities are not available most ministers should be able to help. Essentially, the sermon should consist of an explanation of the meaning of the text in its original context, followed by an application of the message of the passage to the needs and situation of the present.

Alternatives to the sermon may also be considered. Several elders might be asked to make brief statements from their own experience of life, linked to the theme of the readings. Where there is little time for preparation, an extract can be read from a devotional book (see section 8 for titles), perhaps followed by silence or quiet music. Alternatively, there can be the reading of a longer section of the Bible, perhaps a complete chapter from a Gospel.

8   CREED

Where a congregation is accustomed to the use of the Apostles' Creed, this would follow the Proclamation of the Word as an affirmation of the faith of the whole Church.

9   BLESSING

The Blessing of the people from God is a function specifically of the ordained ministry. The service should therefore conclude with a prayer for blessing using the form 'us' rather than 'you'.

Notes

Notes

First Order of Service

1   CALL TO WORSHIP
The leader says
   Let us worship God.

2   HYMN

3   SENTENCES
The leader says
   God is spirit, and those who worship him
   must worship him in spirit and in truth.   (Joh. 4.24)

4   PRAYERS
The leader says
   Let us pray:

   Heavenly Father,
      help us with your good and kindly Spirit.
   Inspire our worship and tell us of your love,
      so that we may share your mercy
      and receive your peace;
   through Jesus Christ our Lord.

   We bring you now our lives as they are,
      our joys and sorrows,
      our hopes and fears.
   There are things that are good in us,
   there are things that are wrong in us,
      and we look to you for healing and encouragement.
                                       ᴧ forgiveness

9

We humbly and honestly admit
    that we have hurt other people and harmed ourselves.
We have missed signs of your providence in the world
    and have lost opportunities of meeting one another's
        needs.
Set us free from guilty memories of things gone wrong,
    and by your kindness and patient love
    change and renew our lives.

As we have been forgiven, so may we forgive;
as we have been welcomed by our heavenly Father,
    so may we practise hospitality of heart and home.
In the days which lie ahead of us,
give us those things which we need
    to make us useful and cheerful disciples;
through Jesus Christ our Lord.

Amen

5 HYMN

6 FIRST READING
The reader says
    The Old Testament reading is written in (. . . *book* . . .),
    chapter (. . . *ab* . . .), verse (. . . *xy* . . .).

7 PSALM
(sung or said)

8 SECOND READING
The reader says
    The Epistle reading is written in (. . . *book* . . .),
    chapter (. . .*ab*. . .), verse (. . . *xy*. . .).

The Gospel reading is written in The Gospel
according to St (. . . *NN* . . .), chapter (. . . *ab* . . .),
verse (. . . *xy* . . .).

At the end of the readings, the reader says
May God bless to us these readings from his holy Word.

Amen

9   HYMN

10   SERMON
A Sermon may be preached

11   OFFERING
The leader says
The Offerings will now be received.

12   PRAYERS
The leader says
Let us pray:

We bring our gifts to you, O God,
in gratitude and hope.
In dedicating them, we dedicate ourselves again
to be your people in the world,
through Jesus Christ our Lord

Almighty and merciful God,
the source of every good and perfect gift,
we praise you for your mercies,
new every morning and renewed in the evening.
Your goodness created us,
your grace sustains us,
your discipline corrects us,

your patience bears with us,
your love redeems us.
We are thankful for all your gifts.
Help us to show our gratitude and love
   by serving you and delighting to do your will;
through Jesus Christ our Lord.

Heavenly Father,
   bless your Church here and throughout the world.
Help all who are called Christians
   to live together in love and unity.
Send your Spirit upon the Church,
   that by word and deed
   she may bring new hope to the world.

Ruler of all,
   we pray for our land and for all lands,
for our Queen and for all heads of state,
   and for those who influence the life of nations.
Help them to rule faithfully and well,
   for the peace of the world and the good of all peoples.

Move our hearts to care
   for the ill, the hungry, and the sorrowful;
that through our love they may
   receive your healing and your strength.

Bless those we love, our families and friends:
   keep them safe from danger,
   and guard them with your peace.

Bless those we do not love,
   those who have offended us, or done us wrong.
Take from our hearts all spite and bitterness,

and help us to live in joyful peace.
Support us when we stumble,
and lead us in the path of truth;
through Jesus Christ our Lord.

God of all times and places,
we remember with joy
all the faithful departed,
especially those whom we have loved.
Bring us with them at the last
to inherit those good things
beyond our imagining and deserving,
which you have prepared for those who love you;
through Jesus Christ our Lord.

Our Father ...   *Amen*

13   INTIMATIONS
The leader says
Here are the Intimations ...

14   HYMN

15   THE PRAYER FOR BLESSING
The leader says
May the blessing of the God of life be ours;
May the blessing of the loving Christ be ours;
May the blessing of the Holy Spirit be ours;
to cherish us, to help us, to make us holy.

Amen

Notes

Second Order of Service

1   CALL TO WORSHIP
The leader says
   Let us worship God.

2   HYMN

3   SENTENCES
The leader says
   Set your minds on things that are above,
   and not on things that are on the earth.
   For your life is hid with Christ in God.

4   PRAYERS
The leader says
   Let us pray:

   Almighty God, whose hidden presence sustains and
   nourishes the world:
   help us now to be open to your coming,
   and speak *to hear* your word of welcome and of peace;
   through Jesus Christ our Lord.

   O God, greater than our thoughts can know,
     higher than our words can tell,
   fill our lives with the sense of your presence,
     that we may be glad of heart,
     and serve you with a quiet mind.

   Merciful God, hold not our sins against us, but forgive.
   Bring us
   new life when we are worn and tired,

new love when we are hard of heart,
new joy when we feel sad in spirit.
Set free our souls from all that holds us down,
    and raise us up to life with Christ again.

Heavenly Father, whose everlasting mercy never fails,
    make us merciful in our dealings with others.
Help us to shape our lives by the pattern of your love,
    and give us the courage and generosity
    to accept other people as they are;
    through Jesus Christ our Lord.

Amen

5   HYMN

6   FIRST READING
The leader says
The Old Testament reading is written in (. . . *book* . . .),
chapter (. . . *ab* . . .), verse (. . . *xy* . . .).

7   PSALM
(sung or said)

8   SECOND READING
The leader says
The Epistle Reading is written in (. . . *book* . . .),
chapter (. . . *ab* . . .), verse (. . . *xy* . . .).

The Gospel Reading is written in The Gospel,
according to St (. . . *NN* . . .), chapter (. . . *ab* . . .),
verse (. . . *xy.* . .).
May God bless to us these readings from his holy Word.

Amen

9   HYMN

10   SERMON
A Sermon may be preached.

11   OFFERING
The leader says
The Offerings will now be received.

12   PRAYERS
The leader says
Let us pray:

O God our Father,
we bring our gifts to you from whom all blessings flow.
Help us with our gifts to bring our lives,
and use us for your glory and the well-being of your people;
through our Lord and Saviour Jesus Christ.

Generous God,
we bring our thanks to you:

for this life and all its blessings,
for joys great and simple,
for gifts and powers more than we deserve,
for the assurance that your mercy knows no limit,
for the presence of Christ in our weakness
and strength,
for the power of Christ to transform our suffering.

In darkness and light,
in trouble and in joy,
help us to trust your love,
to serve your purpose, and
to praise your name;
through Jesus Christ our Lord.

We pray for the life of your Church in all the world.
Make every congregation a community of love,
and every baptised Christian a witness to your grace.
Renew us all who worship in this place,
that we may be a living fellowship of your Spirit,
    serving the parish and the world
        in the name of Christ,
        sharing his love with all.

We pray for the life of the world.
Teach us by the power of your love to live
as members of one human family,
rejecting the things that make for war,
    bearing one another's burdens,
    working together to make a world
        of righteousness and peace;
through Jesus Christ our Lord.

We pray for the life of our country.
Bless your servant Elizabeth our Queen,
    the ministers of the Crown,
    and all members of Parliament.
Guide those who rule among us
    and govern them in your faith and fear.
Protect those who defend our shores and
    guard the peace.
We pray for those who are passing through time of trial:
    through poverty, through ill-health, through deep
        anxiety.
Take from them the spirit of fear,
and give them your spirit of peace and hope.

We pray for those we love, our families and friends.
Strengthen the love we have for them,
and give them all that they need
    for their welfare and happiness.
Let no evil befall them,
and guide them in all their ways;
    through Jesus Christ our Lord.

Eternal God, our Father,
    whose love is stronger than death,
    we rejoice in the communion of your saints.
We remember all who have faithfully lived and died,
    especially those most dear to us,
    who are for ever safe in your love and care.
We pray that we may come with them
    to share in the glory of your eternal kingdom;
    through Jesus Christ our Lord.

Our Father . . .   *Amen*

13 INTIMATIONS
    The leader says
    The following are the Intimations.

14 HYMN

15 THE PRAYER FOR BLESSING
    The leader says
    May the Lord meet in mercy all that seek him.
    May the kindness of the Lord rest and remain upon all
        his people in every land.
    May the Lord hasten his coming,
    and give us all the blessing of peace
        now and for ever.   *Amen*

Notes

Third Order of Service

1 CALL TO WORSHIP
The leader says
It is good for us to be here.

There are many good things in our lives,
and it is right to show gratitude.
There are many worrying things in our lives,
and it is right to look for help.
There are many frightening things within us and around us,
and it is right to seek hope and confidence.

It is a good thing for Christian people,
to be reminded of the things of Christ,
and to see our lives
in relation to the providence and grace
of the God and Father of our Lord.
In a moment of silence let us make ready our hearts for
today's service.

Silence may be kept for about 30 seconds.

2 PRAYERS
The leader says
Let us pray:

Lord of all being, and shepherd of our souls,
lead us in our worship and bless us in the things we say
and think and do,
to your great glory and for the good of all;
through Jesus Christ our Lord.   *Amen*

3 HYMN

4   FIRST READING
    The reader says
        Let us hear of:

        Noah and the Ark,
        in the Book of Genesis, chapter 8, verses 1 to 19
or
        Jacob and his ladder,
        in the Book of Genesis, chapter 28, verses 11 to 22
or
        Joseph and his brothers,
        in the Book of Genesis, chapter 45, verses 1 to 15

        We hear the ancient stories of the presence
            and the purpose of God.
        We look for keener awareness now
            of the mystery of holiness.
        We ask for help to notice holy things,
            and find God's presence in what we see around us

    Silence may be kept for a time

5   PSALM
    (sung or read)

6   SECOND READING
    The reader says
        Let us hear one of the Parables of Jesus:

        the story of the Good Samaritan,
        in St Luke, chapter 10, verses 25 to 37
or
        the story of the Labourers in the Vineyard,
        in St Matthew, chapter 20, verses 1 to 16
or

the story of the Maidens and their lamps,
in St Matthew, chapter 25, verses 1 to 13

Jesus the story-teller catches our attention.
Jesus the poet kindles our imagination.
Jesus the teacher gives us understanding.
Jesus the Son of God reveals the Father's love.

Silence may be kept for a time.

7   HYMN

8   PRAYERS
    The leader says
    Let us pray:

    Let us bless the Lord our God
       for all good things.

    Gracious God, receive our hearty thanks

       for life and love
       for health and food
       for work and home
       for nature's beauty and comfort
       for human skill and laughter
       for memory and hope

    and for things in this past week which have given us
       pleasure and strength and nourishment.

    With grateful hearts
    we offer our thanks and praise,
       in the name and in the spirit of Christ Jesus our Lord,
       in whom we see your everlasting goodness
       and receive your kindly care.   *Amen*

9   THE CREED
     The leader says
          Let us say the Apostles' Creed.

10   HYMN

11   OFFERING

12   INTIMATION

13   PRAYERS
     The leader says
          Let us bring to the Lord
               our concern and commitment, our hopes and worries,
                    in relation to our own lives
                    and the lives of those we love,
               as well as the wider human community of the world.

          Let us seek for ourselves and for others
               the liberating mercy of God,
               to free us from our sense of failure
               and send us forward as new people.

     Silence may be kept for a time

          Let us offer to the Lord
               our interest in this parish and community;
               our awareness of the good that is around us
               as well as the need for better ways.

     Silence may be kept for a time

          Let us commend to the Lord
               our country and every country,

and let us pray for peace and prosperity,
for health and justice, for hope and liberty
in every place on earth.

Silence may be kept for a time.

Good Lord, we bring our loving hopes and prayers
for those we love,
for people in pain,
for all the world.

Silence may be kept for a time

In your great love you set us free from guilt and fear.
Send your kindness flowing through us
and through your whole Church
to serve the purpose of your peace:
through Jesus Christ our Lord.

Our Father . . .   *Amen*

14 HYMN

15 THE GRACE
The leader says
The grace of the Lord Jesus Christ,
and the love of God,
and the fellowship of the Holy Spirit,
be with us all evermore.

Amen

Notes

Fourth Order of Service

1   CALL TO WORSHIP
The leader says
    Let us worship God

2   SENTENCES
The leader says
    Send out your light and your truth
        to be my guide;
    let them lead me to your holy hill,
        to your dwelling place.
    Then I shall come to the altar of God,
        the God of my joy and delight.

3   HYMN
(Hymn 32   'Immortal invisible, God only wise')

4   PRAYERS
The Leader says
    Let us pray:

    God of glory,
    your light fills the world,
    your truth guides your people,
    your love shelters and supports us all.
    May your light shine on us now,
    your truth inspire our words
    and your love reach out through our service to others;
    through Jesus Christ our Lord.

    God of goodness,
    the truth of your love remains constant.

But

Our lives have been untrue,
to you, to others, and ourselves.
Our thoughts, words, and deeds
have lacked faith, hope and love;
and we are troubled by the memory
of things left unsaid and undone.

Silence may be kept for a time

God of grace,
ready and waiting to forgive and restore:
may your Spirit of love in Christ crucified and risen
so fill us with light and hope
that our lives may be lived
to your praise and glory;
through the same Jesus Christ our Lord.   **Amen**

5   HYMN
(Hymn 133 'Break forth, O living light of God')

6   FIRST READING
The reader says
Hear the Word of God.

The Old Testament reading is written in (. . . *book* . . .),
the (. . . *nth* . . .) chapter, at the (. . . *nth* . . .) verse.

At the end of the lesson the reader says:
Thanks be to God.

7   PSALM
(Metrical psalm 19 at 125 in the hymnbook)

8   SECOND READING
The reader says:

The Epistle is written in (. . . *book* . . .), the
(. . . *nth* . . .) chapter, at the (. . . *nth* . . .) verse.

The reader says
    The Holy Gospel is written in (. . . *book* . . .),
    the (. . . *nth* . . .) chapter, at the (. . . *nth* . . .) verse.

At the end of the Second Reading the reader says
    Thanks be to God.

9   THE CREED
The leader says:
    Let us stand and say the Apostles' Creed

or Hymn 414, 'We believe in one true God', may be sung

10   PRAYERS of THANKSGIVING and INTERCESSION
The leader says
    Let us pray:

    Loving God,
    We give thanks for your goodness to us,
    known and unknown:
        for the world with its beauty and mystery,
        for our lives with their promise and past,
        for our loved ones and friends whose company means
            so much to us.
    Above all, we give thanks for Christ Jesus:
        for his love for the outcast and stranger,
        for his care for those troubled in body or mind,
        for his death on the cross and his resurrection,
        for the gift of his Holy Spirit

May we continue to show our gratitude
in the way we live and give glory to you,
Father, Son and Holy Spirit,
one God blessed and glorious for ever and ever.

Holy God,
We pray for the Church in this land,
and for all her parishes and congregations;
that we may be strengthened in our knowledge
and understanding of your truth.
By our words and deeds
may we continue to proclaim
your love with joy and generosity of spirit,
that the world may be led to know you.

We pray for the world,
for peace where there is strife,
for comfort where there is suffering,
and unity where there is discord.
Strengthen by your Spirit,
all who work for the good of others,
through education, relief agencies and governments.

We pray for our country, our Queen, and
her Government;
for those in authority and those with influence;
that working for the common good,
they may serve us
with wisdom, integrity and compassion.

We pray for those who sorrow, those who are in trouble,
for those who suffer cruelty, injustice or neglect.
In their weakness may they share your strength,
and in their despair find hope.

In you, Father, we are one family
   in earth and heaven.
We remember in your presence those who have died,
and give thanks for those
   who revealed to us your grace in Christ.
Help us to follow their example,
   and bring us with them
   to the fullness of your kingdom of love and peace;
through Jesus Christ our Lord.

*If there be no Sermon, the service proceeds to The Prayer
of Dedication (number 15) and continues from there to the
end.*

11   HYMN
   (Hymn 457 'Fill thou our life, O Lord our God')

12   PRAYER FOR ILLUMINATION
   The preacher says
      Let us pray:

      Lord God,
      You have given your word as a lamp to light our way.
      May we receive your truth in faith and love,
      and be strengthened to live as you would have us live,
      to the glory of your name;
      through Jesus Christ our Lord.

13   SERMON
   which concludes with an Ascription of Praise

14   ASCRIPTION OF PRAISE
The preacher says
     To God the Father, God the Son and God the Holy
     Spirit be all praise now and for ever.

15   THE OFFERINGS
The Offerings, if not already gathered, are now received

16   PRAYER OF DEDICATION
The leader says
     Let us pray:

     Lord God,
     grant that our gifts may be used in the service of
          your kingdom,
     through Jesus Christ our Lord.

     Our Father . . .   ***Amen***

17   HYMN
(Hymn 405 'All my hope on God is founded')

18   THE GRACE
The leader says
     The grace of the Lord Jesus Christ,
     the love of God,
     and the fellowship of the Holy Spirit,
     be with us all,
        now and for ever.

                                              Amen

Notes

Notes

Fifth Order of Service

(If possible the Order should be printed to allow participation by the congregation)

1   CALL TO WORSHIP
  Leader   This is the day that God had made:
  People   We will rejoice and be glad in it.

  Leader   Lord, open our lips:
  People   And our mouths shall proclaim your praise.

2   HYMN OF PRAISE

3   PRAYER
  The leader says
    Let us pray:

      We believe, O God, that you are the eternal God of life;
      We believe, O God, that you are the eternal God of love;
      We believe, O God of all the peoples, that you have
            created us
        from dust and ashes.
      O God, who brought us to the joyful light of this day,
      bring us to the guiding light of eternity.

      O God our creator,
      your kindness has brought us the gift of a new day.
      Help us to leave yesterday,
      and not to covet tomorrow,
      but to accept the uniqueness of today.

    (Silence)

By your love, celebrated in your Word,
seen in your Son,
brought near by your Spirit,
take from us what we need carry no longer,
so that we may be free again
to choose to serve you
and to be served by each other.

(Silence)

Leader   Jesus Christ, Son of God, have mercy upon us:
People   Jesus Christ, Son of God, have mercy upon us.

(Silence)

Leader   We believe that God forgives and sets us free,
              and at the day's beginning,
              we commit ourselves to following where Christ
                 calls,
              and to loving one another.
People   We believe that God forgives and sets us free,
              and at the day's beginning,
              we commit ourselves to following where Christ
                 calls,
              and to loving one another.   ***Amen***

4   PSALM
(Read either responsively, or with one or two voices)

5   CHILDREN'S ADDRESS
(if appropriate)

6   HYMN

7   READINGS
   At the end of the readings, the reader says
   This is the word of the Lord

   The people respond
   Thanks be to God.

8   HYMN

9   ADDRESS
   *(Or a reflection on the Word, in the form of dramatised
   reading or mime, meditation or testimony)*

10 OFFERING
   The leader says
   Let us continue to worship God in the giving of an offering

11 PRAYERS
   The leader says
   Let us pray:

       Eternal God,
       you know us, you made us,
       you chose us, you have called us,
       and we are yours.
       By the breath that enlivens us,
       by the love you have shown us,
       by the life that awaits us,
       we receive your promise and know its truth.

       And so we bless you + *praise + thank*
       for the glory of creation,
       for the power of the Word made flesh,
       for the Spirit that transforms us in fellowship,

for the Kingdom you establish within and among us.
We bless you for the Church, your Body,
the mystery of your own creating,
bone of your bone and flesh of your flesh.
And we bless you that you give to us
the task of raising up signs of the Kingdom of love
in the midst, of the kingdoms of the world.

For this place and time,
for the people around us, seen and unseen,
for the promise of live everlasting,
we bless you and thank you, O God.

Your grace is the well-spring of our lives.
Lead us, that we may drink deeply of it.

We thank you. God, for all that is significant for us
at this time.

*(Here, specific thanks may be included, by the leader or
others, or these may be offered in silence.)*

We bring before you, God, the people and situations
concerning us now.

We remember those whose lives are directed towards
destruction instead of creation . . . .

After each part of the prayer silence may be kept.
Then the leader says
Lord, in your mercy
The people say
Hear our prayer

We remember those for whom each day is a burden
   instead of a gift . . .
We remember the sick and those who care for them . . .
We remember those who have no voice, the forgotten
   and the outcast . . .
We remember those whose lives are threatened by
   war, in justice and cruelty . . .
We remember the poor, the homeless and those who see
   no hope . . .
We remember the people of our own community, and
   those who suffer among us . . .
We remember the church throughout the world, and our
   own fellowship of faith . . .
We remember those we love, those who feel unloved,
   and those who cannot love . . .
And as we pray for others, so we pray for ourselves . . .

Lord, set your blessing on us now.
Confirm in us the truth by which we rightly live.
Confront us with the truth from which we wrongly turn.
We ask not for what we want, but for what you know
      we need,
   as we offer our gifts, our prayers and ourselves for you
      and to you,
through Jesus Christ our Saviour.

Our Father . . .   ✓ *inside back cover*   *Amen*

12 HYMN

13 THE GRACE
The leader says
   Let us go out gladly, in the peace and the power of the Spirit.

The people say
    The grace of the Lord Jesus Christ,
    and the love of God,
    and the fellowship of the Holy Spirit,
    be with us all evermore.
                                                    Amen

Notes

Notes

Sixth Order of Service

(This order is based on a Service from India and brings us into fellowship with the world Church)

1   CALL TO WORSHIP
    The leader says
        Let us worship God

2   HYMN

3   SCRIPTURE SENTENCES
    The leader says
        We love the house where you live, O Lord,
            the place where your glory dwells.

4   PRAYERS OF APPROACH
    The leader says
        Let us pray:

        Day after day, O Lord of our lives
        shall we stand before you, face to face?

        With folded hands, O Lord of all the world,
        shall we stand before you, face to face?

        In toilsome cities, filled with the bustle of many people
        shall we stand before you, face to face?

        Under your great sky, in solitude and silence,
        with humble heart,
        shall we stand before you, face to face?

And when our work in this world is done,
   O King of Kings,
alone and speechless, shall we stand before you
   face to face?   *(Rabindranath Tagore)*

Almighty God, most blessed and most holy,
before whose brightness the angels veil their faces,
with honour and with adoring love we come to worship you.
May your pure light shine in our hearts and
open the eyes of our understanding,
that we may worship you more fully in heart and mind;
through Jesus Christ our Lord.

Amen

5   HYMN

6   PRAYERS of ADORATION and CONFESSION
The leader says
   Let us pray:

   O Lord our God,
   we praise you for the wonder of your creation,
   for the precious gift of life,
   and for sending your Son to bring us to fullness of life.
   We bless you for his holy incarnation,
   for his perfect life on earth,
   for his suffering for us and his triumph over death,
   for his ascension to your right hand
   and his gift of the Holy Spirit,
   and for the promise of his coming again.

People
   Holy God, holy and mighty, holy and immortal,
   have mercy upon us.

Leader

O my people, what have I done to you, or wherein have I wearied you? Answer me.

Because I brought you forth out of the land of Egypt, and led you to a land exceeding good;
you have prepared a cross for your Saviour.

People

Holy God, holy and mighty, holy and immortal,
have mercy upon us.

Leader

Before you, I opened the sea;
and with a spear you have opened my side.
I went before you in a pillar of cloud;
and you have brought me to the judgement hall of Pilate.

People

Holy God, holy and might, holy and immortal,
have mercy upon us.

Leader

I fed you with manna in the desert;
and you have beaten me with blows and stripes.
I made you to drink the water of salvation from the rock;
and you have made me to drink gall and vinegar.

People

Holy God, holy and mighty, holy and immortal,
have mercy upon us

Leader

I gave you a royal sceptre;
and you have given my head a crown of thorns.

I lifted you up with great power;
and you have hung me upon the gibbet of the cross.

People
Holy God, holy and mighty, holy and immortal,
have mercy upon us

Leader
Lord have mercy
People
Christ have mercy
Leader
Lord have mercy

Lord, open to us today the sea of your mercy
and water us with full streams from the riches of your
grace
and springs of your kindness.
Make us children of quietness and heirs of peace;
kindle in us the fire of your love;
sow in us your fear;
strengthen our weakness by your power
and bind us close to you and to each other,
in Christ's name.   ***Amen***

7   FIRST READING
(From the Epistles)

8   SECOND READING
(From the Gospel)

9   ADDRESS

10   OFFERING

The leader says
> The Offerings will now be received

11   HYMN

12   PRAYERS of THANKSGIVING and INTERCESSION

The leader says
> Let us pray:

Leader
> Lift up your hearts

People
> We lift them up to the Lord

Leader
> Let us give thanks to our Lord God

People
> It is right to give him thanks and praise

Leader
> King of the ages and giver of all holiness,
> you are holy, and holy in your son, Jesus Christ our Lord,
> and holy also is your Holy Spirit, who searches all things.
>
> You made us out of dust, and gave to us the delight
> of paradise.
> And when we broke your commands, you did not
> despise or forsake us,
> but called us by your law and instructed us by your
> prophets.
>
> And in the fullness of time you sent your only Son,
> who being born a man by the Holy Spirit and the
> Virgin Mary,
> renewed your image in humankind.

Risen, blessed Lord, we bring before you the needs of
the world.
Remember, O Lord, our family and friends

(Silence)

Remember, O Lord, the sick and the suffering

(Silence)

Remember, O Lord, the hungry and the oppressed

(Silence)

And rejoicing in the communion of saints,
we remember with thanksgiving before you
all who have faithfully lived and died.

Keep us in unbroken fellowship with the whole church
in heaven and on earth,
through Jesus Christ our Lord,
who lives and reigns and is glorified with you,
Father and Holy Spirit for ever.   ***Amen***

Our Father . . .   ***Amen***

13   HYMN

14   THE PRAYER FOR BLESSING
The leader says
Great light of the world,
impart to us the richness of your blessing,
the fullness of life that you alone can give.
And the blessing of God almighty, Father, Son and Holy
Spirit, be with us all evermore.

Amen

Notes

Notes

Additional Prayers

NOTE: It has not been possible to trace the origins of all the various threads which form the tapestry of the prayers that follow. The rhythms and patterns, the expression and phrases, the ideas and images, have all been woven from many different sources, and are acknowledged with gratitude.

APPROACH

1   Heavenly Father,
      we make a silence for your worship.
      In the stillness, show yourself to us.

    We have come
      to worship you
      in your glory and your love,
      to thank you for your goodness to us,
      and to offer you our obedient faithful service.

    Come to us, Lord,
    and teach us a new way of living
    in deeper faith and greater love;
      through Jesus Christ your Son.

2   O God:
     we know that you are everywhere,
     but now we bring ourselves into your presence.

     We have come here
       to praise you,
       to thank you,
       to worship you,
       to listen to you.

     Grant that we may
       stay by your side this day,
       and walk with you all the days of our life;
       through Jesus Christ our Lord.

3   O God of wonder and of joy,
     come now and dwell with us.

     When we are weak, give us strength;
     when we are unhappy, give us courage;
     when we are puzzled, show us the way.

     Help us to find our greatest joy
       in knowing that you are beside us.
     As we go forward,
       may the light of your hope shine in our eyes,
     and faith and love possess our hearts;
       through Jesus Christ our Lord.

4   O God, unseen but present,
          give us a calm mind and a quiet spirit
              that we may hear you speak.
          Show us what we must do,
              for you, for others, for ourselves;
          and help us do it now, and do it gladly;
              through the power of Jesus Christ your Son.

5   O God of truth and love:
          open our eyes to the glory of your presence;
          attune our ears to the sound of your voice;
          loosen our tongues in the joy of your worship;
          and fill our lives with wonder, love, and praise;
              through Jesus Christ our Lord.

6   God of light and peace,
          we look for your coming among us with joy:
          may our lives be transformed by your presence.

      Attune us to your voice,
              to your silence;
          that we may receive the word of your peace.

      As we wait in your presence,
          fill our minds with your thoughts,
              our hearts with your desires,
              our hands with your love;
                  through Jesus Christ our Lord.

CONFESSION

1   Heavenly Father,
        you never go away from us
        but we so often go away from you.
        We are sorry for our faults,
            for the unkindness that causes pain to others
            and cuts us off from you.

    Forgive us all our sin,
        and give us grace
        to live closely to your guiding hand,
            now and always.

2   O God of mercy and of grace,
        you know the secrets of our hearts:
            how blind we are to our own faults,
                how harsh we are in judging others;
            how swift we are to take for gain,
                how slow we are to give for others;
            how proud we are of our success,
                how ready to break faith with others.

    Do not remember our sins and offences,
    but remember us in your unfailing love,
        in accordance with your goodness;
            through Jesus Christ our Lord.

3   Father in heaven,
        your love brings
            life to dead souls,
            light to darkened minds,
            strength to weak wills.

Help us to believe and trust
that no wrong we have done,
no good we have failed to do,
is too great for you to pardon,
through the merits
of Jesus Christ your Son.

4   O God, our heavenly Father,
pardon the wrong we have thought and
said and done.
Forgive our selfishness and greed,
our stubbornness and pride,
our idleness and ease.

Cleanse us and save us,
for the sake of Christ your Son;
and by his Spirit
help us to love you more
and to serve you better.

5   O God,
give us grace to make a fresh start today.

We know we have not loved you with our
whole heart,
nor have we loved our neighbours as ourselves.

As we hope to be forgiven,
teach us also to forgive;
and lead us forward in a new life
where neither grudges nor resentment
have a part;
through Jesus Christ our Lord.

ILLUMINATION
(Before Sermon)

1   O God,
        you have revealed to us the light that is eternal.

     Open our eyes
        that we may see your purpose for our lives,
     and give us obedience in the things we know
        that fresh light may shine upon our way.

     So shall we walk the path of life without stumbling,
     because we are illuminated by your presence.

2   Enlighten us by your Spirit,
        O God of light and truth;
           that no careless mind,
              no callous heart,
              no casual will
           may block the entrance of your word into
              our lives.

     Come in the full richness of your power
        to confirm us in penitence,
           raise us in hope,
           strengthen us for service;
        and fill us with the true knowledge of your Son,
        Jesus Christ our Lord.

3   Grant us, O Lord,
        to listen for your word
           with eager faith,

with brimming hope,
and with love that kindles knowledge;
through Jesus Christ our Lord.

4   There is no darkness in you, O God.

Send forth your light into our hearts,
that we may see the shining glory of your word,
and walk with joy the path you set before us.

5   Show your love to us, O God,
through Jesus Christ your Son;
and may his Spirit, through your word,
make us strong to love and serve one another.

DEDICATION OF THE OFFERING

1   Accept, O Lord,
          the offering we seek to make,
              of ourselves and our possessions;
          and grant that we may ever work and pray
              to build a world of peace
              and joy and freedom;
                  through Jesus Christ our Lord.

2   O God, from whom all blessings flow,
          receive the offerings which now we make
          for the honour of your Name
          and the glory of your Kingdom.

3   O God,
          as we bring our offerings to you,
          we dedicate ourselves to your service.

          By our study of your word
              may we strengthen our faith;
          by our prayers for your Church,
              may we further her work;
          by love for our neighbours,
              may we honour your Name;
                through Jesus Christ our Lord.

4   Lord God,
          all that we are and all that we have
          is your gift to us.

Our gifts and prayers,
and the whole of our lives,
we offer with joy to your service;
    through Jesus Christ, your Son, our Lord.

5   We bring our gifts to you, O God,
        with cheerfulness and a joyful heart.

Grant that with our gifts,
    we may also offer
        a ready mind and a willing spirit
            to show forth in our lives
                the truth of the Gospel;
                    through Jesus Christ.

DISCIPLESHIP AND SERVICE

1   Almighty God,
        through Jesus Christ your Son
           you call us to refuse the evil and to choose
             the good.
           Grant us eagerness to hear his teaching,
             readiness to obey his commandments,
               and devotion to give ourselves to his service,
                 with no reserve and no delay.

2   O Lord Jesus Christ,
        take our hands and work with them;
        take our lips and speak through them;
        take our minds and think with them;
        take our hearts and set them on fire
           with love for you and all your people;
             for your Name's sake.

3   O God, the Lord of all good life,
        we thank you for your joyous gifts
           of love and peace and gladness of heart.
    We ask you now for courage,
        that we may do what is right,
           and find in the joy of serving others
           the joy of serving you;
             through Jesus Christ our Lord.

4   Lord God,
        by whose power we are created,
        by whose love we are redeemed:

guide and strengthen us by your Spirit,
that we may give ourselves to your service,
and live in love for one another and for you;
through Jesus Christ our Lord.

5   Lord,
lead us in the way you want us to go,
and give us joy on the way.

6   Loving God,
your Son came not to be served but to serve.
Give us your Spirit.
that we may be ready to give ourselves in your
    service,
not counting the cost and never drawing back.

7   O God,
in Jesus Christ your Son
you have given yourself completely.
Help us by your grace
    to give ourselves as generously
    to you and to one another.

8   O God,
give us grace
    to walk in your light
    and to work for your truth;
    that we who are the children of light,
    may bear witness to you
    at all times and in all places,
by proclaiming your goodness
and practising your Gospel;
through Jesus Christ our Lord.

THANKSGIVING

1   God of all time and space,
         Creator of all things:
              we thank and praise you.

     For your love which created us,
         your power which upholds us,
         your wisdom which guides us:
              we thank and praise you.

     For the good things you give us,
         the beauty you show us,
         the truth you share with us:
              we thank and praise you.

     May the thoughts of our minds,
         the prayers of our hearts,
         the deeds of our lives:
              all thank and praise you.

2   Almighty God, fountain of all mercies,
     we thank you for your goodness and loving-kindness
              to us and to all people.

     We bless you for creating us,
         for keeping us in safety,
              and for blessing us so richly in this life.

     But above all, we thank you for your boundless love
         in redeeming the world by our Lord Jesus Christ,
              for the means of grace, and for the hope of glory.

Give us such a sense of all your mercies
    that our hearts may be truly thankful,
    and that we show forth your praise,
        not only with our lips but in our lives,
        by giving up ourselves to your service,
        and by walking before you in holiness
        and righteousness all the days of our life;
            through Jesus Christ our Lord.

3   We acclaim you, O God, for you are the Lord.

    You brought the universe into being from nothing.
    You created life by your Spirit,
        and made us in your image.
    You sent Jesus your Son to save us from sin,
        and to re-make us in your likeness.
    You fill the hearts of your faithful people
        with light and strength and love,
            to be your Church in the world.
    With the Church in every age and in all places,
        and with the whole company of heaven:

    We acclaim you, O God, for you are the Lord.

4   Almighty God,
        your strong hand set the stars in space,
        your wisdom guides their ordered paths.

        Your steadfast love created us,
        your power directs our daily lives.

With all creation we rejoice,
and praise your providence divine.

Confirm our faith, awaken hope,
and keep us in the light of love.

5 God of grace and God of glory,
  all light flows from you,
  all line and shape and colour.

We thank you for the gift of sight,
 by which we look with joy
 on all the works of your hand.

Grant us clear eyes and pure hearts,
 that we may read your writing everywhere
 in the pages of your creation.

6 Almighty God, Creator of all,
  the heavens sing your glory,
  the earth and sea and sky proclaim your might.

> AMR
4/6

We thank you for the loveliness we hear
 in the many voices of creation,
 in the singing of birds and the call of beasts,
 in the rhythms of running water,
 in the sighing of wind in trees,
 in the laughter of children and friends.

Grant that we may ever hear in them
 the music of your love and goodness;
  through Jesus Christ our Lord.

INTERCESSIONS
(General)

1   God of mercy and of grace,
    we are not worthy to ask you for anything,
    yet you encourage us to pray for others,

May your mercy rest upon your Church,
    that she may abound in peace and truth, in unity and
        service.

Grant grace to the Queen,
    and help her always to be your servant,
    that both she and those who hold office under her,
    may do all things well, to your glory and honour.

Remember all our friends, and those with whom we find
    it hard to be friendly.
Give power to the weak, strength to the poor,
    comfort to the sad, healing to the sick;
and bring us all to your eternal Kingdom.

2   Heavenly Father,
    bless your Church in every land,
        and grant that Christians everywhere
        may live together in love and unity.
    Bless our country and our Queen,
        and all in positions of responsibility,
        that we may be your people, and you may be our
           God.

Bless all who are homeless, hungry, or unhappy,
   and move us to be your helping hands to care for them.

Bless all who defend our shores and guard the peace,
   and those whose daily work is dangerous,
   that your protection and our gratitude
   may give them courage.

Bless those who are dear to us, at home or far away,
   that neither time nor distance may weaken
   the love that binds us together.

All this we ask in the Name of Jesus Christ,
   your Son, our Lord.

3   Remember, O Lord, your people throughout the world.
   May Christ so rule our lives
   that we may give ourselves
     in the service of others
     and in witness to your truth.

Remember, O Lord, the nations of the world.
   Give understanding to their leaders,
   and wisdom to their peoples,
     that co-operation and community
     may be established everywhere.

Remember, O Lord, the needy of the world.
   Show them your power to save,
   and give them cause to believe in your love.

Remember, O Lord, those who have done us good,
   and those who have done us harm.

Deliver them from all that can hurt the soul,
    and bring us with them at the last
    into the joy and fellowship of your heavenly Kingdom.

4   For the peace of the world,
    the welfare of the Church,
    the unity of all peoples:
        let us pray to the Lord.

(Silence to be kept)

For the Queen and her government,
    the leaders of the world,
    and all in authority:
        let us pray to the Lord.

(Silence to be kept)

For those who are oppressed,
    the destitute and hungry,
    the unemployed and those who have less than we
        because of injustice:
        let us pray to the Lord.

(Silence to be kept)

For those whom we love, at home or far away,
    neighbours and friends and colleagues at work,
    all whose lives are closely linked with ours:
        let us pray to the Lord.

(Silence to be kept)

5   O God of might and power:

Give peace to the nations,
    that they may obey your will.
Comfort all who have lost heart,
    and lift up the lonely and cast down
Give help to the poor,
    and to those who are hungry or persecuted.

Bring healing to the sick, strength to the suffering,
    and your presence to the lonely.

And teach those of us who have plenty
    to share your gifts with others;

        through Jesus Christ our Lord.

6   O Lord of wisdom, love, and power:

Guide those who govern
that they may seek your justice and show your mercy.

Give hope to those who are persecuted,
that they may stand firm in the evil day.
Give comfort to those who mourn the loss of a loved
one through death or alienation,
that their hurt may be healed.

Renew those who lack purpose in life,
    or who are uncertain about their faith,
that they may come to trust you more.

Strengthen those who are called by your Name
that here and everywhere they may serve and please
you in word and deed.

Surround our families and friends with your love,
that they may fall into no sin, neither run into any danger.

7   Almighty and everlasting God,
          whose loving-kindness embraces all the world,
               hear our prayers for others.

We pray for those who work for peace and justice,
     that they may know your strength.

We pray for those who suffer from loss of hope or
          purpose,
     that they may know your comfort.

We pray for those who seek to heal and reconcile,
     that they may know your patience.

We pray for those who feel the pain of anger, hurt, or
          bitterness,
     that they may know your peace.

We pray for those whoses cries for help we cannot hear,
     that they may know the courage of your presence.

8   Lord Jesus Christ,
        we acknowledge your rule over every realm of life:
        subdue the world by the might of your love.

     Son of Mary:
        consecrate our homes.
     Son of David:
        cleanse our politics.
     Son of Man:
        rule the nations.
     Son of God:
        grant us eternal life.

     Jesus the Carpenter:
        hallow our daily work.
     Jesus the Saviour:
        save us from ourselves.
     Jesus the Life-giver:
        renew your Church.

     Jesus the Crucified:
        reveal your love and power to all who suffer.
     Jesus the King:
        raise us to live and reign with you for ever.
     Jesus the Word of God:
        perfect your creation,
        and bring the world to the knowledge of your love:

     For the Kingdom, the power, and the glory are yours,
        for ever and ever.

9   Heavenly Father:
     Remember in your goodness and care
     all whom we love, our families and friends,
     and those who help and cheer us.

     Remember all who are homeless or hungry,
     who are prisoners or hostages,
     who are persecuted for their race, or colour, or belief.

     Remember all who are ill, at home or in hospital.
     all who are lonely and sad,
     especially . . . .

     Remember all who find their work dreary or dull,
     and all who have no real work to do.

     We pray that all who are in any kind of trouble
     may know that you are with them,
     and that they may find
     courage and peace, comfort and hope.

INTERCESSIONS
(Particular)

1   Lord God,
>your Son Jesus Christ worked in the carpenter's shop
>   in Nazareth:
>we pray for those whose work is useful and
>   satisfying,
>for all who have tedious and unrewarding jobs to do,
>and for those who are unemployed and have little
>   prospect of work.
>Grant that there may be a fuller sharing of job
>   opportunities,
>and understanding and co-operation in industrial
>   relations.
>So may we learn to work,
>not for gain, but for one another,
>and for a just society,
>for Jesus' sake.

2   Eternal God,
>by your creative power the universe was made,
>and humankind endowed with intelligence to explore it.
>We pray for those whose scientific skills
>make it possible to travel into space
>and probe infinity.
>May space research be guided by profound respect
>for the integrity of creation,
>that planet earth may be preserved
>as a home for future generations,
>and the universe resound with praise for you
>through Jesus Christ our Lord.

3   God our Father,
         your Son taught us to love one another.
         In a world of fear and hostility between nations and
              races,
         give us grace to love others,
         to appreciate the gifts which other races bring to us,
         and to see in all people
         our brothers and sisters
         for whom Christ died.
         Save us from prejudice
         or arrogance to those who are different from us.
         And grant that we may inherit the freedom
         of the children of God
         through Jesus Christ our Lord.

4   Almighty God,
         your Son had nowhere to lay his head:
         have compassion on those who are homeless
         or who live in overcrowded conditions
         or as squatters.
         Give them strength and hope
         and keep them close to you.
         Enable us to work and pray
         for the day when all your children
         are housed and healthy
         and free to live full and happy lives,
         for Jesus' sake.

5   Almighty God,
           your Son brought healing to the sick and hope to the
               despairing:
           We pray for all who suffer from illnesses
           for which there is no cure.
           Surround them with love and care.
           Bless doctors and nursing staff
           and prosper the work of those engaged in research.
           And grant that those who suffer
           may know the fellowship of Christ
           who bore pain and suffering for us,
           and at the last won victory over death,
           to whom be glory for ever.

6   Eternal God,
           your Holy Spirit leads into all truth:
           we pray for your blessing on the work of
           schools and colleges and universities.
           Grant that all who learn
           and all who teach
           may be united in seeking truth
           and furthering knowledge,
           and may come to know you as the source of all wisdom,
           through him who is the way, the truth, and the life,
           even Jesus Christ our Lord.

7   Eternal Lord God,
           you are the source of all beauty and harmony:
           we praise you for every way in which the arts reflect
               your truth
           and lift up the human spirit.
           We thank you for the inspiration of artists and authors,

composers and directors;
for the skill and imagination of performers;
and for the powers by which we are enabled
to enjoy and appreciate artistic expression.

Grant that lives may be enriched
and your name glorified
through the power of truth.

8   God our Father,
      your Son fed the bodies as well as the souls of people:
      we bring before you the needs of all who suffer
      from hunger and poverty in the world today.
      Forgive us for allowing injustice to continue
      and safeguarding our own standard of living.
      Lead the international community to seek
      justice for the poorer nations,
      an end to unfair trade,
      and aid that will bring real development.
      So make us all to be sisters and brothers,
      caring for one another
      as members of one human family,
      for Jesus' sake.

9   God our Father,
      your Son Jesus Christ was the child of refugee parents:
      we pray for all children who suffer from conflict
            and deprivation:
      for those who live on the streets of war-torn cities,
      for those made homeless or orphans by violent change,
      and for those who will never know anything but
            disease and hunger.

To your great compassion we commend all such
        fragile lives.
Give us an active sympathy for all who suffer
and bless those who work for the welfare of children
        in any kind of need
for the sake of the Christ child.

10   Almighty God,
        your Son came to be the Prince of Peace:
        we pray for grace that we may follow in his ways
        and may know the happiness of those who are
                peacemakers.
        Direct by your Holy Spirit
        statesmen and national leaders
        and international organisations,
        that the barriers of fear and suspicion
        between people and nations may crumble,
        and all people,
        recognising their common humanity,
        may be united in seeking justice and peace
        for Jesus' sake.

NOTES ON ADDITIONAL PRAYERS

Approach
1   adapted from Bell (57)
2   ibidem (55)
3   ibidem (47, 42)
4   adapted from Evening Service No 5 (POW)
5   adapted from Acland (Trinity 12)
6   unknown

Confession
1   adapted from Bell (92)
2   unknown
3   adapted from Evening Service No 5 (POW)
4   compilers
5   adapted from Bell (93)

Illumination
1   adapted from Evening Service No 2 (POW)
2   adapted from a prayer of George Adam Smith
3   adapted from E Milner-White
4   adapted from Bell (52)
5   unknown

Dedication of the Offerings
1-5   unknown/compilers

Discipleship and Service
1   adapted from Acland (Trinity 5)
2   adapted from Commonwealth Youth Sunday (POW)
3   adapted from Loretto Services (53)
4-8   unknown/compilers

Thanksgiving
1   adapted from Bell (5, 6, 9)
2   adapted from the General Thanksgiving
3   adapted from *The Divine Service* (POW)
4   suggested by Bell (1)
5   adapted from Bell (11)
6   adapted from Bell (10)

Intercessions (General)
1   adapted from Bell (61)
2   adapted from Bell (62)
3   adapted from Commonwealth Youth Sunday (POW)
4   adapted from Loretto Services (p 13)
5   adapted from Loretto Services (p 16)
6   adapted from Loretto Services (p 19)
7   adapted from Loretto Services (p 22)
8   adapted from an Ecumenical Service (BCC)
9   adapted from Bell (60

Intercessions (Particular)
1-5   compilers

SOURCES

Prayers for Every Day, edited by Vicars Bell, OUP, 1965.
Ninety Four Collects for the Christian Year, Eric Milner-White,
SPCK, 1956.
Loretto Chapel Services of Worship and Prayers.
A Service for Ecumenical Occasions, British Council of Churches.
*Orders of Evening Service, Order for Commonwealth Youth
Sunday,* and *Prayers for Divine Service,* are all published by
the Church of Scotland Committee on Public Worship and
Aids to Devotion.

Notes

Notes

Hymns

1 The arrangement of items in the following Praise Lists follows the order in which the hymns are arranged in *Church Hymnary: Third Edition* (CH3).

2 Provision is made for congregational singing in six places in the service, though normally only five items may be required, and on occasion perhaps only four.

3 Those items printed *in italics* are intended for use when Holy Communion is celebrated, though they may be used at other times. Item VI is often brief, sometimes no more than a doxology. A children's hymn is offered for each Sunday.

4 A suggestion is offered in each list for one of the items to be taken from *Songs of God's People*.

5 The numbers of psalms, prose psalms with CH3 numbers, and paraphrases, are printed **in bold type**. Prose psalms and canticles are also offered as alternatives at II or III. A fuller selection of psalms, both for singing and reading, is provided in the next section.

6 The calendar of the Christian Year and the suggested themes come from *The Book of Common Order (1979)*.

7 No provision is made for evening worship. Evening hymns are gathered in CH3 at 50-59, and 641-656.

8 Provision is made for Christmas Eve, Holy Week, and other occasion.

Notes

Ninth Sunday before Christmas

The Creation

I	9	Praise to the Lord, the Almighty, the King of Creation (**138**, 33)
II	**70**	O, hear my prayer, Lord (77, **102**)
III	141	O Lord of every shining constellation (120, 148, 151, 494, PP 8)
IV	**135**	(1-5) The Lord of heaven confess (149, 428, 367)
V	*586*	*Father, we thank thee who hast planted*
VI	**135**	(6), (32, 578 (5))
CH	151	God, who made the earth
SGP	37	Great is thy faithfulness

30	(1-6) All creatures of our God and King (35)
95	O Light that knew no dawn (118)
147	God moves in a mysterious way (**137**, 163)
143	The spacious firmament on high (33, 144, 146)
566	*The earth belongs unto the Lord*
30	(7), (437)
153	A little child may know
70	Lord, bring the day to pass

Eighth Sunday before Christmas

The Fall

I	**23**	God shall endure for aye (31)
II	104	Come, Holy Spirit, come (**64, 65**)
III	**125**	God's law is perfect, and converts (PP 145)
IV	238	Praise to the Holiest in the height (388, 439, 452, 461)
V	*580*	*And now, O Father, mindful of the Love*
VI	362	From all that dwell below the skies (588)
CH	448	Just as I am, thine own to be
SGP	113	We lay our broken world

34	Lord of all being, throned afar (**70, 71**)
114	Christ, whose glory fills the skies (**68**, 83)
150	When all thy mercies, O my God (PP 53)
371	O for a thousand tongues, to sing (377, 460)
437	*Love Divine, all loves excelling*
660	Unto God be praise and honour (**590**)
435	Lord, in the fulness of my might
115	What a friend we have in Jesus

Seventh Sunday before Christmas

The Election of God's People: Abraham

I	39	Stand up, and bless the Lord (43)	382		All hail, the power of Jesus' name
II	**71**	O God, give ear unto my cry (**75**, 106)	110		O thou who camest from above (113, 161)
III	358	The God of Abraham praise (163)	431		Jesus, Master, whose I am (**333**)
IV	498	Arm of the Lord, awake, awake	471		Lift up your heads, ye gates of brass (444, 669)
V	*570*	*I am not worthy, holy Lord*	*571*		*Jesus, thou Joy of loving hearts*
VI	463	Forth in thy Name, O Lord, I go	617		(4) To Father, Son, and Holy Ghost (483)
CH	426	A glorious company we sing	112		Jesus Christ, I look to thee
SGP	106	Those who wait upon the Lord	69		Look forward in faith

Sixth Sunday before Christmas

The Promise of Redemption: Moses

I	2	Before Jehovah's awesome throne (9)	37		Praise the Lord! ye heavens, adore him
II	86	I greet thee, who my sure Redeemer art (**101**)	**393**		When Zion's bondage God turned back (**73**)
III	**8**	I love the Lord, because my voice (337, 147, 345)	364		King of glory, King of peace (121, 163)
IV	**396**	Behold the amazing gift of love (409, 499)	397		O God thou art the Father (299)
V	*355*	*God reveals his presence*	*572*		*Come, risen Lord, and deign to be our guest*
VI	658	Praise God, from whom all blessing flow	659		All praise and thanks to God (358)
CH	427	The Church is wherever God's people are praising	97		Father, lead me, day by day
SGP	95	Sing of the Lord's goodness	36		God who is everywhere present on earth

Fifth Sunday before Christmas

The Remnant

I	**136**	Praise ye the Lord; for it is good	7	O send thy light forth and thy truth (**19**)
II	76	Dear Lord and Father of mankind (**66, 67**)	90	Lead us, heavenly Father, lead us (**73**)
III	357	Eternal light! eternal light	674	Jesus, these eyes have never seen (**349**)
IV	405	All my hope on God is founded (**393**)	**394**	Art thou afraid his power shall fail (668)
V	575	*(1-4) Thou standest at the altar*	400	*Firmly I believe and truly*
VI	**532**	Hark how the adoring hosts above *(575 (5))*	472	(i) Fear not, thou faithful Christian flock
CH	97	Father, lead me, day by day	501	Far round the world thy children sing their song
SGP	24	Do not be afraid	90	One more step along the world I go

Fourth Sunday before Christmas (Advent I)

The Advent Hope

I	165	O come, O come, Emmanuel (36, **311**)	165	O come, O come, Emmanuel (**160**)
II	**333**	Thou shalt arise, and mercy yet (62)	**294**	How glorious Zion's courts appear (PP 85)
III	323	'Thy Kingdom come!' – on bended knee (397)	320	Come, thou long-expected Jesus
IV	313	Christ is coming! let creation (223)	316	Lo! he comes, with clouds descending (437)
V	324	*Blest is the man, O God*	566	*(4-5) Ye gates, lift up your heads on high* (314)
VI	325	From glory to glory advancing, we praise thee, O Lord (**590**)	296	(1 and 5) Rejoice, the Lord is King
CH	502	God of heaven, hear our singing	419	Lord, I would own thy tender care
SGP	67	Maranatha	120	You shall go out with joy

Third Sunday before Christmas (Advent II)

The Word of God in the Old Testament

I	25	Only on God do thou, my soul (**41**)	27	Ye righteous, in the Lord rejoice (**312**, 12)
II	122	Come, Holy Ghost, our hearts inspire (**127, 159**)	11	Jesus, stand among us (**125**, PP 40)
III	128	Book of books, our people's strength (130, PP 19)	133	Break forth, O living light of God (129, 130)
IV	496	O Spirit of the living God (495, 535)	372	Ye servants of God, your Master proclaim (373, 476, 519)
V	577	*Let all mortal flesh keep silence*	518	*(1-5) Forth from on high the Father sends*
VI	301	(4) Glory to God the Father	657	Now to him who loved us *(581 (6))*
CH	124	Holy Spirit, hear us		
SGP	45	How lovely on the mountains	132	(1-3) Tell me the old, old story
			51	In a byre near Bethlehem

Second Sunday before Christmas (Advent III)

The Forerunner

I	208	On Jordan's bank the Baptist's cry (315)	321	The Lord will come and not be slow (**26**)
II	511	O day of God, draw nigh (324)	508	Almighty Father, who dost give
III	320	Come, thou long-expected Jesus (162, 161)	121	Thou art the Way: to thee alone (PP 37 (1-18)
IV	316	Lo! he comes, with clouds descending (323, 505, 408)	318	Mine eyes have seen the glory (319, 445, 317)
V	585	*According to thy gracious word*	577	*Let all mortal flesh keep silence*
VI	351	(1-2 and 6) O thou my soul, bless God the Lord	339	O Breath of life, come sweeping through us *(588)*
CH	417	God is always near me	419	Lord, I would own thy tender care
SGP	103	The voice of God goes out	74	Lord, to whom shall we go?

First Sunday before Christmas (Advent IV)

The Annunciation

I	38	Songs of praise the angels sang (12, **346**)	**160**		Hark, the glad sound! The Saviour comes (46)
II	13	Light of the anxious heart (164, PP 80)	7		O send thy light forth and thy truth (163)
III	170	It came upon the midnight clear (**167**)	113		Blest are the pure in heart (404)
IV	669	Put thou thy trust in God (681)	505		Christ is the world's true light (317, 454, 460)
V	*511*	*O Day of God, draw nigh*	*582*		*(1-7) In love, from love, thou camest forth, O Lord*
VI	165	O come, O come, Emmanuel	313		Christ is coming! let creation *(582 (8))*
CH	98	Jesus, Saviour ever mild	227		I love to hear the story
SGP	88	O what a gift	96		Sing we a song of high revolt

Christmas Day

The Birth of Christ

I	191	O come, all ye faithful	190		Christians, awake, salute the happy morn
II	180	Child in the manger	175		Angel voices, richly blending
III	195	Away in a manger, no crib for a bed (189)	202		How brightly beams the morning star (184)
IV	179	See! in yonder manger low (**390**)	194		Love came down at Christmas
V	*172*	*(1, 3 and 4) O little town of Bethlehem*	*583*		*Lord, enthroned in heavenly splendour*
VI	169	Hark! the herald angels sing (183 (2-3))	198		(1-2 and 5) Of the Father's love begotten
CH			195		Away in a manger, no crib for a bed
SGP	11	Before the world began	1		A holy baby

First Sunday after Christmas

The Wise Men

I	198	(1-4) Of the Father's love begotten (38)
II	**168**	The race that long in darkness pined
III	175	Angel voices, richly blending (182, 187, 188, **166**)
IV	200	As with gladness men of old (425, 194)
V	582	*(1-7) In love, from love, thou camest forth, O Lord*
VI	198	(5) Christ, to thee, with God the Father *(582 (8))*
CH	464	The wise may bring their learning
SGP	46	Humbly in your sight

40	Worship the Lord in the beauty of holiness (179)
167	His large and great dominion shall (62)
202	How brightly beams the morning star (201, 173)
199	Bethlehem, of noblest cities (425, 494, 196, 507)
579	*Almighty Father, Lord most high*
660	Unto God be praise and honour *(204)*
488	Jesus bids us shine, with a pure, clear light
87	Oh the life of the world

Second Sunday after Christmas

The Presentation in the Temple

I	22	O sing a new song to the Lord (**348**, 615, **102**, 612)
II	524	Thy Kingdom come; yea, bid it come (148, **158**)
III	205	"Jesus!" Name of wondrous love (206)
IV	373	To the Name of our Salvation (371, 440)
V	**565**	*(1-3) I'll of salvation take the cup*
VI	611	O God, our help in ages past (513, *204, 565 (4)*)
CH	112	Jesus Christ, I look to thee
SGP	92	Praise the Lord

The Visit to Jerusalem

27	Ye righteous, in the Lord rejoice (**347**, 613, 611, 616)
477	Rise up, O men of God (**489**, 105, PP 122)
207	Behold a little Child
397	O God, thou art the Father (405)
570	*I am not worthy, holy Lord*
661	Laud and honour to the Father (614, *589*)
156	I love to think that Jesus saw (309)
17	By cool Siloam's shady rill

Third Sunday after Christmas

The Baptism of Christ

I	208	On Jordan's bank the Baptist's cry (**41**)
II	114	Christ, whose glory fills the skies (317, 104, 161)
III	111	Jesus, good above all other (223, 209, PP 27)
IV	496	O Spirit of the living God (352, 369)
V	568	*Father most loving, listen to thy children*
VI	640	Praise ye the Lord, ye servants of the Lord (*590*)
CH	418	Jesus loves me! this I know
SGP	1	A holy baby

346	O Lord, thou art my God and King (**351**)
95	O Light that knew no dawn (115, 103)
208	On Jordan's bank the Baptist's cry (**284**)
334	Holy Spirit, ever living (364, 378, 681, 402)
565	*(1-3) I'll of salvation take the cup*
635	Almighty God, thy word is cast *(565 (4))*
385	It is a thing most wonderful
81	Now through the grace of Christ

Fourth Sunday after Christmas

The First Disciples

I	**493**	Lord bless and pity us
II	211	Jesus calls us! O'er the tumult (76, 110)
III	322	Thy Kingdom come, O God (PP 111)
IV	447	Lord and Master, who hast called us (445, 430)
V	400	*(1-4) Firmly I believe and truly*
VI	400	Firmly I believe (*400 (5)*)
CH	230	When Jesus saw the fishermen
SGP	23	Come with me, come wander

9	Praise the Lord, the Almighty, the King of Creation
127	Teach me, O Lord, the perfect way
323	'Thy Kingdom come!' – on bended knee (497, PP 97)
422	City of God, how broad and far (211, 593)
567	*Deck thyself, my soul, with gladness*
669	Put thou thy trust in God (486)
123	Hushed was the evening hymn
118	Will you come and follow me?

Fifth Sunday after Christmas

The First Sign

The Wedding at Cana

I	9	Praise to the Lord, the Almighty, the King of Creation
II	43	Father, we praise thee, now the night is over (**5**, 306)
III	209	How vain the cruel Herod's fear (83, 345, **598**)
IV	421	Glorious things of thee are spoken (408, 457)
V	*577*	*Let all mortal flesh keep silence*
VI	634	May the grace of Christ our Saviour (74 (6))
CH	465	Hands to work and feet to run
SGP	10	As man and woman we were made

The New Temple

	10	Christ is made the sure foundation (**4**)
	119	Enter thy courts, thou Word of life (113, 109)
	295	Where high the heavenly temple stands (163, 420)
	294	How glorious Zion's courts appear (437, 405, **346**, 674)
	572	*Come, risen Lord, and deign to be our guest*
	532	(1-2 and 5) Hark how the adoring hosts above
	16	Lord Jesus, be thou with us now
	49	I will enter his gates (59)

Sixth Sunday after Christmas

The Friend of Sinners

I	**101**	Give priase and thanks unto the Lord (77)
II	667	Approach, my soul, the mercy-seat (104, **136**)
III	663	O for a closer walk with God (215, PP 84)
IV	431	Jesus, Master, whose I am (409, 686, 669)
V	*570*	*I am not worthy, holy Lord*
VI	371	O for a thousand tongues, to sing (37)
CH	100	Jesus, Friend of little children
SGP	33	God forgave my sin

Life for the World

	1	All people that on earth do dwell (12, 11)
	82	One who is all unfit to count (48, 62)
	218	There's a widenss in God's mercy (212)
	496	O Spirit of the living God (437, 432)
	580	*And now, O Father, mindful of the love*
	359	Praise the Lord, his glories show
	633	Little birds in winter time
	25	Dona nobis pacem in terra

Ninth Sunday before Easter

Christmas the Teacher

I	**29**	To render thanks unto the Lord	34	Lord of all being, throned afar
II	110	O thou who camest from above (129)	114	Christ, whose glory fills the skies (691)
III	**127**	Teach me, O Lord, the perfect way (PP 119 (137-152))	128	Book of books, our people's strength (PP 119 (1-16))
IV	400	(1-4) Firmly I believe and truly (371)	428	Lord of creation, to thee be all praise (485)
V	*573*	*(1-4) Here, O my Lord, I see thee face to face*	*577*	*Let all mortal flesh keep silence*
VI	400	(5), *(573 (4-7))*	658	Praise God, from whom all blessings flow
CH	229	I like to think of Jesus	58	If I come to Jesus
SGP	51	In a byre near Bethlehem	93	Seek ye first

Eighth Sunday before Easter

Christ the Healer

I	**23**	God shall endure for aye; he doth	24	God is our refuge and our strength
II	88	God of grace and God of glory	84	Turn back, O man, forswear thy foolish ways (81)
III	**351**	O thou my soul, bless God the Lord (345)	215	Jesus, whose all-redeeming love (219, PP 48)
IV	214	Thine arm, O Lord, in days of old (376)	371	O for a thousand tongues, to sing
V	*569*	*The bread of life, for all men broken*	*570*	*I am not worthy, holy Lord*
VI	657	Now to him who loved us, gave us	659	All praise and thanks to God
CH	228	Jesus' hands were kind hands, doing good to all	17	Serve the Lord with joy and gladness
SGP	112	We cannot measure how you heal	82	O Christ the healer

Seventh Sunday before Easter

Christ, Worker of Miracles

I	36	The Lord is King! lift up thy voice	31	Father most holy, merciful and loving (**28**)
II	**74**	Show me thy ways, O Lord (62)	87	Be thou my Vision, O Lord of my heart
III	133	Break forth, O living light of God	220	O sing a song of Bethlehem (PP 122)
IV	519	Judge Eternal, throned in splendour	492	O thou who at thy Eucharist didst pray
V	*587*	*Author of life divine*	*578*	*Now, my tongue, the mystery telling*
VI	361	Let all the world in every corner sing	637	Come, dearest Lord, descend and dwell
CH	419	Lord, I would own thy tender care	18	This is God's holy house
SGP	63	Let the world unite and	31	Gabi, Gabi

Sixth Sunday before Easter (Lent I)

The King and the Kingdom: Temptation

I	77	Father of heaven, whose love profound	**25**	Only on God do thou, my soul (667)
II	**64**	O God, be gracious to me in thy love (PP 51 (1-17))	76	Dear Lord and Father of mankind (PP 130)
III	210	Forty days and forty nights	676	Hark, my soul! it is the Lord
IV	96	Thou hidden Love of God, whose height	415	The great love of God is revealed in the Son
V	*414*	*We believe in one true God*	*440*	*'Lift up your hearts!' We lift them, Lord, to thee*
VI	660	Unto God be praise and honour	**312**	(1-3) Behold! the mountain of the Lord
CH	435	Lord, in the fullness of my might	97	Father, lead me, day by day
SGP	52	Standing in the need of prayer	19	Blessing and honour, wisdom and wealth

Fifth Sunday before Easter (Lent II)

The King and the Kingdom: Conflict

I	109	Spirit of God, that moved of old	**71**	O God, give ear unto my cry (**69**)
II	79	Just as I am, without one plea (45, PP 55)	83	Rock of Ages, cleft for me
III	256	Sing, my tongue, how glorious battle	**396**	Behold the amazing gift of love (PP 62)
IV	415	The great love of God is revealed in the Son	404	God is my strong salvation (406)
V	*352*	*(1-3) Holy, holy, holy, Lord God Almighty*	*581*	*Forth from on high the Father sends*
VI	352	(4)	390	(4) To Father, Son, and Holy Ghost
CH	448	Just as I am, thine own to be	98	Jesus, Saviour ever mild
SGP	62	Lead us, O Father, in the paths of peace	113	We lay our broken world (61)

Fourth Sunday before Easter (Lent III)

The King and the Kingdom: Suffering

I	**65**	Lord, from the depths to thee I cried	72	O God of Bethel! by whose hand
II	85	O for a heart to praise my God	216	What grace, O Lord, and beauty shone
III	486	Lover of souls and Lord of all the living (484, PP 86)	469	God, your glory we have seen in your Son (163, 478)
IV	477	Rise up, O men of God	363	Ye holy angels bright
V	*585*	*According to thy gracious word*	*582*	*In love, from love, thou camest forth, O Lord*
VI	32	(1, 3-4) Immortal, invisible, God only wise	658	Praise God, from whom all blessings flow
CH	450	Saviour, teach me, day by day	99	Father, we thank thee for the night
SGP	44	How good it is	18	By the waters of Babylon

Third Sunday before Easter (Lent IV)

The King and the Kingdom: Transfiguration

(Mothering Sunday)

I	6	Thy mercy, Lord, is in the heavens	4	How lovely is thy dwelling-place
II	80	Lord Jesus, think on me	95	O Light that knew no dawn (PP 119 (25-40))
III	217	O wondrous type, O vision fair (PP 77)	217	O wondrous type, O vision fair
IV	537	Jerusalem the golden (490)	397	O God, thou art the Father (535)
V	578	*Now, my tongue, the mystery telling*	584	*Thee we adore, O hidden Saviour, thee (577)*
VI	437	Love Divine, all loves excelling (**590**)	**294**	How glorious Zion's courts appear (589)
CH	222	Wise men seeking Jesus	100	Jesus, Friend of little children
SGP	36	God who is everywhere present	89	Oh, the love of my Lord

Second Sunday before Easter (Passion)

The King and the Kingdom: Victory of the Cross

I	256	(1-4) Sing, my tongue, how glorious battle	238	Praise to the Holiest in the height
II	82	One who is all unfit to count (83, 62)	242	Alone, thou goest forth, O Lord (86)
III	224	My song is love unknown	253	O Sacred Head, sore wounded (**231**)
IV	258	We sing the praise of him who died (301 (1-3), 254, 380)	372	Ye servants of God, your Master proclaim (296 (1-4), 257, 255)
V	574	*Bread of the world, in mercy broken (583)*	576	*O Christ, who sinless art alone (575)*
VI	256	(5), (301 (4))	657	Now to him who loved us, gave us (296 (5))
CH	385	It is a thing most wonderful	112	Jesus Christ, I look to thee
SGP	47	Lord of the dance	8	Hallelujah! My Father

First Sunday before Easter (Palm)

The Way of the Cross

I	233	All glory, laud, and honour	233	All glory, laud, and honour
II	320	Come, thou long-expected Jesus	113	Blest are the pure in heart
III	**73**	I waited for the Lord my God (PP 62)	**390**	O greatly blest the people are (163, **232**)
IV	363	Ye holy angels bright	510	Lord of light, whose Name outshineth
V	*564*	*Mine hands in innocence, O Lord (566 (4-5))*	**565**	*I'll of salvation take the cup*
VI	234	Ride on! ride on in majesty (588)	234	Ride on! ride on in majesty
CH	235	Hosanna, loud hosanna	236	Children of Jerusalem
SGP	42	Here hangs a man discarded	66	Lifted high on your cross

Easter Day

The Resurrection of Christ

I	264	(1-3) Jesus Christ is risen today (**263**, 291)	267	The day of resurrection (275, 273 (1-5))
II	266	The strife is o'er, the battle done (272, 62)	271	This joyful Eastertide
III	274	The world itself keeps Easter Day (**387**)	277	O sons and daughters, let us sing (**351**, PP 118 (19-29))
IV	37	Praise the Lord! ye heavens adore him	359	Praise the Lord, his glories show
V	**566**	*The earth belongs unto the Lord (268)*	*269*	*Come, ye faithful, raise the strain*
VI	264	(4), (167 (4-6))	273	(6) To Father, Son, and Holy Ghost (299 (1, 3 and 5))
CH	280	Good Joseph had a garden	282	Come, ye children, sing to Jesus
SGP	5	Alleluia! (6, 38)	100	Surrexit Dominus

First Sunday after Easter

The Upper Room Appearances

I	265	The Lord is risen indeed
II	**41**	Lord, thee my God, I'll early seek (89, 161)
III	276	Easter glory fills the sky (278)
IV	378	O Jesus, King most wonderful
V	270	*Good Christian men, rejoice and sing*
VI	**135**	(1, 5-6) The Lord of heaven confess
CH	281	At Eastertime the lilies fair
SGP	91	Our Lord Christ hath risen (7)

The Bread of Life

	263	O set ye open unto me
	11	Jesus, stand among us
	270	Good Christian men, rejoice and sing (**8**, 674, PP 150)
	368	Now thank we all our God
	571	*Jesus, thou Joy of loving hearts (567)*
	639	Now may he who from the dead
	151	God, who made the earth
	57	Jesus the Lord said (28, 32, 65)

Second Sunday after Easter

The Emmaus Road

I	6	Thy mercy, Lord, is in the heavens
II	121	Thou art the Way: to thee alone
III	93	Loving Shepherd of thy sheep (345)
IV	397	O God thou art the Father
V	572	*Come, risen Lord, and deign to be our guest*
VI	**395**	Father of peace, and God of love
CH	153	A little child may know
SGP	39	Halleluya! We sing your praises

The Good Shepherd

	38	Songs of praise the angels sang
	114	Christ, whose glory fills the skies (672, PP 3)
	530	Blest be the everlasting God (163)
	381	I will sing the wondrous story (388)
	492	*O thou, who at thy Eucharist didst pray*
	393	(1-2 and 5) When Zion's bondage God turned back
	93	Loving Shepherd of thy sheep
	20	Christ is alive

Third Sunday after Easter

The Lakeside			**The Resurrection and the Life**	
I	15	We love the place, O God	46	This is the day of light
II	78	Jesus, Lover of my soul	78	Jesus, Lover of my soul
III	220	O sing a song of Bethlehem (PP 29)	**26**	The Lord's my light and saving health (278, PP 27)
IV	279	Thine be the glory, risen conquering Son	605	Jesus lives! thy terrors now
V	*575*	*Thou standest at the altar*	*276*	*Easter glory fills the sky*
VI	362	From all that dwell below the skies	657	Now to him who loved us, gave us
CH	154	All things bright and beautiful	156	I love to think that Jesus saw
SGP	72	Lord Jesus Christ	40	He is Lord

Fourth Sunday after Easter

The Charge to Peter			**The Way, the Truth and the Life**	
I	**29**	To render thanks unto the Lord	**101**	Give praise and thanks unto the Lord
II	111	Jesus, good above all other	292	Away with gloom, away with doubt
III	**139**	I to the hills will lift mine eyes (PP 8)	302	Jesus, our hope, our heart's desire (PP 26)
IV	495	O Lord our God, arise!	121	Thou art the Way: to thee alone
V	*497*	*God of mercy, God of grace*	*586*	*Father, we thank thee who hast planted*
VI	**390**	O greatly blest the people are	457	(1-2 and 4) Fill thou our life, O Lord our God
CH	99	Father, we thank thee for the night	309	O Son of Man, our Hero strong and tender
SGP	54	Jesus calls us here to meet him	53	It's no life

Fifth Sunday after Easter

Going to the Father

I	36	The Lord is King! lift up thy voice	**136**		Praise ye the Lord; for it is good
II	**101**	Give praise and thanks unto the Lord	151		God, who made the earth
III	304	Join all the glorious names (297, PP 123-124)	**394**		Art thou afraid his power shall fail (PP 118 (1-18))
IV	301	(1-3) Christ is the world's Redeemer (318)	296		Rejoice, the Lord is King
V	582	*In love, from love, thou camest forth, O Lord*	585		*According to thy gracious word*
VI	301	(4)	659		All praise and thanks to God
CH	386	Praise him, praise him, all ye little children	157		We thank thee, God, for eyes to see
SGP	94	Sing alleluia to the Lord	119		You are worthy

Sixth Sunday after Easter

The Ascension of Christ

I	286	The Head that once was crowned with thorns	289	Look, ye saints! the sight is glorious
II	48	O Lord of life, thy quickening voice (62)	108	Spirit of God, descend upon my heart (62)
III	**285**	Thou hast, O Lord, most glorious (**284, 294,** PP 47)	**566**	The earth belongs unto the Lord (295, 221, PP 24)
IV	305	Sing we triumphant hymns of praise (299, 300)	297	All praise to thee, for thou, O King divine (298)
V	581	*Forth from on high the Father sends (582, 583, 288)*	576	*O Christ, who sinless art alone (287, 307, 290, 56)*
VI	382	All hail, the power of Jesus' Name (301 (1 and 3-4), 308)	**293**	The Saviour died, but rose again (589 (1-2))
CH	383	Come, children, join to sing	418	Jesus loves me! this I know
SGP	75	Majesty, worship his majesty	55	Jesus is Lord!

Pentecost

The Gift of the Spirit

I	342	Come, Holy Ghost, our souls inspire (328)
II	320	Come, thou long-expected Jesus
III	**348**	Sing a new song to Jehovah (327, **326**, PP 98)
IV	514	Eternal Ruler of the ceaseless round
V	7	*O send thy light forth and thy truth (570, 276)*
VI	364	King of glory, King of peace (329 (1 and 5))
CH	124	Holy Spirit, hear us
SGP	4	All over the world (105)

107	Spirit Divine, attend our prayers (329, 330)
11	Jesus, stand among us (332)
331	When God of old came down from heaven (PP 68 (1-20))
341	How great the harvest is
338	*Spirit of mercy, truth and love (334)*
678	Thee will I love, my Strength, my Tower
386	Praise him, praise him, all ye little children
98	Spirit of the Living God (104)

First Sunday after Pentecost (Trinity) (St Columba)

The Riches of God

I	352	(1-3) Holy, holy, holy, Lord God Almighty (31)
II	**136**	Praise ye the Lord; for it is good
III	336	Our blest Redeemer, ere he breathed (335, 345)
IV	354	Glory be to God the Father (401)
V	564	*Mine hands in innocence, O Lord (578)*
VI	352	(4), (**395**, 494)
CH	152	How wonderful this world of thine
SGP	35	God the Father of Creation (58)

The Church's Message

402	I bind unto myself today (43, 32)
122	Come, Holy Ghost, our hearts inspire (87, 90)
301	Christ is the world's Redeemer (288, 61, 212, 339, PP 97)
397	O God thou art the Father (398, **391**, 377, 372)
571	*Jesus, thou Joy of loving hearts*
473	Lord, who in thy perfect wisdom (635)
426	A glorious company we sing
43	Holy, holy, holy is the Lord

Second Sunday after Pentecost

The People of God

I	10	Christ is made the sure foundation (**28**)
II	113	Blest are the pure in heart
III	334	Holy Spirit, ever living (PP 8)
IV	**390**	O greatly blest the people are (421, **347**)
V	**565**	*I'll of salvation take the cup*
VI	**530**	Blest be the everlasting God (491)
CH	488	Jesus bids us shine, with a pure, clear light
SGP	26	Father, we adore you

The Church's Unity and Fellowship

19	O come, and let us to the Lord
103	Breathe on me, Breath of God (117)
140	The Lord doth reign, and clothed is he (133, PP 118 (19-29))
420	The Church's one foundation (422, 424)
492	*O thou, who at thy Eucharist didst pray*
489	I joy'd when to the house of God (474)
427	The Church is wherever God's people are praising
13	Bind us together (77)

Third Sunday after Pentecost

The Life of the Baptised

I	9	Praise to the Lord, the Almighty, the King of Creation
II	88	God of grace and God of glory (**74**, 91)
III	**138**	How excellent in all the earth (305, PP 46)
IV	**333**	Thou shalt arise, and mercy yet (341)
V	580	*And now, O Father, mindful of the love*
VI	429	My God, accept my heart this day
CH	230	When Jesus saw the fishermen
SGP	81	Now through the grace of Christ

The Church's Confidence in Christ

6	Thy mercy, Lord, is in the heavens (**23**)
104	Come, Holy Spirit, come
241	There is a green hill far away (306, PP 107 (1-22))
413	Jesus shall reign where'er the sun (373, **396**, 405)
573	(1-4) Here, O my Lord, I see thee face to face
505	Christ is the world's true light *(573 (5-7), 500, 483)*
383	Come, children, join to sing
14	Blessed assurance

Fourth Sunday after Pentecost

The Freedom of the Sons of God

I	34	Lord of all being, throned afar
II	114	Christ, whose glory fills the skies (90, 95)
III	337	For thy gift of God the Spirit (304, 163)
IV	**396**	Behold the amazing gift of love (379, 406, 407, 410)
V	*584*	*Thee we adore, O hidden Saviour, thee*
VI	463	Forth in thy Name, O Lord, I go (431, 445, 636)
CH	418	Jesus loves me! this I know
SGP	71	Lord God, your love has called us

The Church's Mission to the Individual

2	Before Jehovah's awesome throne
105	Come, thou Holy Paraclete (94, 665, 62)
338	Spirit of mercy, truth and love (**139**)
371	O for a thousand tongues, to sing (374, 376, 409)
570	I am not worthy, holy Lord
494	Thou whose almighty word (496, *588*)
416	God is love: his the care
3	Abba, Father

Fifth Sunday after Pentecost

The New Law

I	**19**	O come, and let us to the Lord
II	106	Holy Spirit, Truth Divine (92, 161)
III	339	O Breath of life, come sweeping through us (144)
IV	**346**	O Lord thou art my God and King (378, 408)
V	*566*	*The earth belongs unto the Lord*
VI	457	Fill thou our life, O Lord our God (397, *590*, 497)
CH	348	Sing a new song to Jehovah
SGP	2	A new commandment

The Church's Mission to all Men

1	All people that on earth do dwell
115	Come down, O Love Divine (107)
340	Spirit of Light – Holy (300, 303, PP 147)
382	All hail, the power of Jesus' Name (424, 456, 475)
586	Father, we thank thee who hast planted
476	'For my sake and the Gospel's go (**493**, 495, *589*)
501	Far round the world thy children sing their song
27	Father, we love you (108)

Sixth Sunday after Pentecost

The New Man

I	35	O worship the King all-glorious above
II	48	O Lord of life, thy quickening voice
III	**139**	I to the hills will lift mine eyes (PP 121)
IV	437	Love Divine, all loves excelling
V	568	*Father most loving, listen to thy children*
VI	**167**	(4-6) His Name for ever shall endure
CH	16	Lord Jesus, be thou with us now
SGP	102	The Spirit lives to set us free (71)

4	How lovely is thy dwelling-place
108	Spirit of God, descend upon my heart (PP 63)
220	O sing a song of Bethlehem
369	God and Father, we adore thee
572	*Come, risen Lord, and deign to be our guest*
658	Praise God, from whom all blessings flow
229	I like to think of Jesus
117	When our lives are joined to Christ

Seventh Sunday after Pentecost

The More Excellent Way

I	2	Before Jehovah's awesome throne
II	115	Come down, O Love Divine (PP 34 (1-18))
III	**225**	Ye who the Name of Jesus bear
IV	415	The great love of God is revealed in the Son (438)
V	570	*I am not worthy, holy Lord*
VI	9	(2-4) Praise to the Lord, who o'er all things so wondrously reigneth
CH	17	Serve the Lord with joy and gladness
SGP	84	O Lord, all the world belongs to you

40	Worship the Lord in the beauty of holiness
109	Spirit of God, that moved of old (PP 42)
216	What grace, O Lord, and beauty shone
437	Love Divine, all loves excelling (459)
580	*And now, O Father, mindful of the love*
637	Come, dearest Lord, descend and dwell
450	Saviour, teach me, day by day
109	Ubi caritas

Eighth Sunday after Pentecost

The Fruit of the Spirit

I	19	O come, and let us to the Lord	9	Praise to the Lord, the Almighty, the King of Creation
II	106	Holy Spirit, Truth Divine (62)	342	Come, Holy Ghost, our souls inspire (105)
III	334	Holy Spirit, ever living	492	O Thou, who at thy Eucharist (425, 420, 163)
IV	341	How great the harvest is	505	Christ is the world's true light
V	*352*	*Holy, holy, holy, Lord God Almighty*	*577*	*Let all mortal flesh keep silence*
VI	359	(1-2) Praise the Lord his glories show	659	All praise and thanks to God
CH	18	This is God's holy house	151	God, who made the earth
SGP	101	The God of heaven is present	104	There's a spirit in the air

Ninth Sunday after Pentecost

The Whole Armour of God

I	4	How lovely is thy dwelling-place	36	The Lord is King! lift up thy voice
II	87	Be thou my Vision, O Lord of my heart	91	Defend me, Lord, from hour to hour (88)
III	443	Who would true valour see (345)	404	God is my strong salvation (**26**)
IV	441	Soldiers of Christ! arise (481)	478	Soldiers of the cross, arise (477)
V	*353*	*Round the Lord in glory seated*	*351*	*(1-5) O thou my soul, bless God the Lord*
VI	362	From all that dwell below the skies	351	(6)
CH	49	The morning bright, with rosy light	153	A little child may know
SGP	87	Oh the life of the world	110	We are marching in the light of God

Tenth Sunday after Pentecost

The Mind of Christ

I	40	Worship the Lord in the beauty of holiness	35	O worship the King all-glorious above
II	95	O Light that knew no dawn	110	O thou who camest from above (PP 56)
III	216	What grace, O Lord, and beauty shone (397, PP 48)	**225**	Ye who the Name of Jesus bear (506, 461, 432)
IV	373	To the Name of our Salvation (259, 297)	460	O, brother man, fold to thy heart thy brother
V	*355*	*God reveals his presence*	*364*	*King of glory, King of peace*
VI	639	Now may he who from the dead	640	Praise ye the Lord, ye servants of the Lord
CH	226	I can picture Jesus toiling	228	Jesus' hands were kind hands, doing good to all
SGP	76	Make me a channel of your peace	19	Christ be beside me

Eleventh Sunday after Pentecost

The Serving Community

I	1	All people that on earth do dwell	46	This is the day of light
II	110	O thou who camest from above (104)	511	O Day of God, draw nigh (PP 36)
III	442	Fight the good fight with all thy might (131)	515	Father, who on man dost shower (218, 453)
IV	510	Lord of light whose Name outshineth (PP 145)	366	Sing to the Lord a joyful song
V	*572*	*Come, risen Lord, and deign to be our guest*	*579*	*Almighty Father, Lord most high*
VI	657	Now to him who loved us, gave us	**167**	(4-6) His name for ever shall endure
CH	465	Hands to work and feet to run	427	The Church is wherever God's people are praising
SGP	21	Christ's is the world	16	Blessing and honour, wisdom and wealth

Twelfth Sunday after Pentecost

The Witnessing Community

I	36	The Lord is King! lift up your voice	**23**	God shall endure for aye; he doth	
II	**125**	God's law is perfect, and converts (62)	130	Lord, thy word abideth	
III	468	Speak forth thy word, O Father (470)	512	Where cross the crowded ways of life (163)	
IV	509	O Holy City, seen of John (514, 505)	471	Lift up your heads, ye gates of brass (685, 686)	
V	584	*Thee we adore, O hidden Saviour, thee*	575	*Thou standest at the altar*	
VI	637	Come, dearest Lord, descend and dwell (589)	657	Now to him who loved us, gave us (588)	
CH	449	Looking upward every day	426	A glorious company we sing	
SGP	34	Go tell everyone	22	Colours of day	

Thirteenth Sunday after Pentecost

The Suffering Community

I	38	Songs of praise the angels sang	7	O send thy light forth and thy truth	
II	241	There is a green hill far away (PP 39)	86	I greet thee, who my sure Redeemer art (80)	
III	**591**	I'm not ashamed to own my Lord	491	Lord of our life, and God of our salvation (**489**, PP 92)	
IV	259	In the cross of Christ I glory	297	All praise to thee, for thou, O King divine (238)	
V	587	*Author of life divine*	568	*Father most loving, listen to thy children*	
VI	659	All praise and thanks to God	463	Forth in thy Name, O Lord, I go (639)	
CH	435	Lord, in the fullness of my might	385	It is a thing most wonderful	
SGP	48	I need thee every hour	79	Nada te turbe	

Fourteenth Sunday after Pentecost

The Neighbour

I	29	To render thanks unto the Lord		37	Praise the Lord! ye heavens adore him
II	88	God of grace and God of glory (122)		133	Break forth, O living light of God (PP 82)
III	461	O God of mercy, God of might (PP 33)		436	O Master, let me walk with thee
IV	360	Praise, my soul, the King of heaven (503, 460, 526)		96	Thou hidden Love of God, whose height (512, 525, 527)
V	574	*Bread of the world, in mercy broken*		581	*Forth from on high the Father sends*
VI	371	(1-2 and 6) O for a thousand tongues, to sing		660	Unto God be praise and honour
CH	466	Our thoughts go round the world		464	The wise may bring their learning
SGP	41	Help us accept each other		60	Fill us with your love

Fifteenth Sunday after Pentecost

The Family

I	9	Praise to the Lord, the Almighty, the King of Creation		107	Spirit Divine, attend our prayers
II	113	Blest are the pure in heart (141)		90	Lead us, heavenly Father, lead us (134)
III	523	O happy home, where thou art loved the dearest (213, 345)		522	Our Father, by whose Name (524, PP 120/121)
IV	368	Now thank we all our God (370)		367	For the beauty of the earth (145, 447)
V	581	*Forth from on high the Father sends*		583	*Lord, enthroned in heavenly splendour*
VI	354	Glory be to God the Father		658	Praise God, from whom all blessings flow
CH	99	Father, we thank thee for the night		98	Jesus, Saviour ever mild
SGP	10	As man and woman we were made		36	God who is everywhere present

Sixteenth Sunday after Pentecost

Those in Authority

I	46	This is the day of light	10	(1-3) Christ is made the sure foundation
II	120	Lord of beauty, thine the splendour	121	Thou art the Way: to thee alone
III	322	Thy Kingdom come, O God (161)	323	'Thy Kingdom come!' – on bended knee (PP 115)
IV	520	O God of earth and altar (321)	519	Judge Eternal, throned in splendour (446, 513)
V	576	*O Christ, who sinless art alone*	571	*Jesus, thou Joy of loving heart*
VI	37	Praise the Lord, ye heavens adore him	10	(4)
CH	100	Jesus, Friend of little children	419	Lord, I would own thy tender care
SGP	103	The voice of God goes out (96)	84	O Lord, all the world belongs to you (62)

Seventeenth Sunday after Pentecost

The Proof of Faith

I	**136**	Praise ye the Lord; for it is good	29	To render thanks unto the Lord
II	122	Come, Holy Ghost, our hearts inspire (62)	110	O thou who camest from above (115)
III	214	Thine arm, O Lord, in days of old (436)	358	The God of Abraham praise (163)
IV	422	City of God, how broad and far	405	All my hope on God is founded
V	**565**	*I'll of salvation take the cup*	578	*(1-4) Now, my tongue, the mystery telling*
VI	640	Praise ye the Lord, ye servants of the Lord	635	Almighty God, thy word is cast *(578 (5))*
CH	154	All things bright and beautiful	226	I can picture Jesus toiling
SGP	107	Through the love of God	116	When our confidence is shaken

Eighteenth Sunday after Pentecost

The Offering of Life

I	107	Spirit Divine, attend our prayers	390	O greatly blest the people are
II	86	I greet thee, who my sure Redeemer art (84)	122	Come Holy Ghost, our hearts inspire
III	223	O Love, how deep, how broad, how high (399, PP 62)	457	Fill thou our life, O Lord our God (445, PP 135)
IV	487	And did those feet in ancient time (486, 479, 451)	485	Lord, speak to me, that I may speak (356, 403, 462)
V	*573*	*(1-4) Here, O my Lord, I see thee face to face*	*569*	*The bread of life, for all men broken*
VI	634	May the grace of Christ our Saviour *(573 (5-7))*	362	From all that dwell below the skies (458)
CH	467	Take our gifts, O loving Jesus	465	Hands to work and feet to run
SGP	46	Humbly in your sight	97	Sons and daughters of creation

Nineteenth Sunday after Pentecost

The Life of Faith

I	32	Immortal, invisible, God only wise	44	Most glorious Lord of Life, that on this day (42 (1-4))
II	85	O for a heart to praise my God	95	O Light that knew no dawn (78)
III	693	My soul, there is a country (537, PP 103)	415	The great love of God is revealed in the Son (411, 345)
IV	423	Through the night of doubt and sorrow	372	Ye servants of God, your master proclaim
V	**351**	*O thou my soul, bless God the Lord*	*355*	*God reveals his presence*
VI	374	To God be the glory! great things he hath done	658	Praise God, from whom all blessings flow (42 (5))
CH	155	God who put the stars in space	228	Jesus' hands were kind hands, doing good to all
SGP	64	Let us go the house of God	9	Amazing grace

Twentieth Sunday after Pentecost

Citizens of Heaven

I	22	O sing a new song to the Lord	28	Praise waits for thee in Zion, Lord
II	80	Lord Jesus, think on me	96	Thou hidden Love of God, whose height
III	409	And can it be, that I should gain (345)	543	Let saints on earth in concert sing (544, PP 24)
IV	400	Firmly I believe and truly	319	Ye servants of the Lord (363)
V	352	*(1-3) Holy, holy, holy, Lord God Almighty*	353	*Round the Lord in glory seated*
VI	352	(4)	**530**	Blest be the everlasting God (**590**)
CH	157	We thank thee, God, for eyes to see	386	Praise him, praise him, all ye little children
SGP	15	Bless the Lord, my soul	83	O happy day

Twenty-first Sunday after Pentecost

Endurance

I	27	Ye righteous, in the Lord rejoice	41	Lord, thee my God, I'll early seek
II	89	Guide me, O thou great Jehovah (673, 682, 62)	114	Christ, whose glory fills the skies (482, 677, 679)
III	535	O what their joy and their glory must be (539, 540)	442	Fight the good fight with all thy might (545, 163)
IV	430	'Take up thy cross,' the Saviour said (434, 304)	413	Jesus shall reign where'er the sun (476, 479, 365)
V	582	*In love, from love, thou camest forth, O Lord*	585	*According to thy gracious word*
VI	361	Let all the world in every corner sing	368	Now thank we all our God
CH	58	If I come to Jesus	383	Come, children, join to sing
SGP	50	I will sing (31)	95	Sing of the Lord's goodness (3)

Christian Unity

I	**489**	I joy'd when to the house of God
II	211	Jesus calls us! O'er the tumult
III	543	Let saints on earth in concert sing (420, PP 133/134)
IV	505	Christ is the world's true light (492)
V	*586*	*Father, we thank thee who hast planted*
VI	634	May the grace of Christ our Saviour (589)
SGP	56	Jesus, stand among us (111)

10	(1-3) Christ is made the sure foundation
88	God of grace and God of glory (PP 122)
490	Jesus, with thy Church abide
422	City of God, how broad and far (**566** (1-3))
572	*Come, risen Lord, and deign to be our guest*
10	(4), (84, 473)
102	The Spirit lives to set us free

Springtime

I	30	(1-5) All creatures of our God and King
II	618	The glory of the spring how sweet (35, 120)
III	619	By the rutted roads we follow (**626**, 150, PP 104)
IV	375	Fairest Lord Jesus
V	*586*	*Father, we thank thee who hast planted*
VI	620	We plough the fields, and scatter
CH	152	How wonderful this world of thine (621)
SGP	87	Oh the life of the world

35	O worship the King all-glorious above (620, **617**)
367	For the beauty of the earth
628	Fountain of mercy, God of love (145, **393**, PP 65)
278	Now the green blade riseth from the buried grain
572	*Come, risen Lord, and deign to be our guest*
635	Almighty God, thy word is cast
622	In the lanes and in the parks
78	Morning has broken

Harvest Festival

I	30	All creatures of our God and King
II	120	Lord of beauty, thine the splendour
III	**617**	Good unto all men is the Lord (142, PP 65)
IV	**387**	The Lord's my Shepherd (627, 620)
V	**566**	*The earth belongs unto the Lord (587)*
VI	366	Sing to the Lord a joyful song (638)
CH	630	The fields and vales are thick with corn
SGP	73	Lord of life (70)

	620	We plough the fields, and scatter (35)
	101	Give praise and thanks unto the Lord
	145	O Lord of heaven and earth and sea (149, PP 24)
	628	Fountain of mercy, God of Love (629, 30 (1-4))
	586	*Father, we thank thee who hast planted*
	339	O Breath of life, come sweeping through us (30 (7))
	631	We thank thee, Lord, for all thy gifts
	37	Great is thy faithfulness

Michaelmas (29th September)

I	8	I love the Lord, because my voice (38)
II	108	Spirit of God, descend upon my heart (117)
III	442	Fight the good fight with all thy might (**135**, PP 104)
IV	353	Round the Lord in glory seated (406, 404, 443)
V	577	*Let all mortal flesh keep silence*
VI	542	(1-3 and 6) Sing Alleluia forth in duteous praise (498)
SGP	85	O Lord, hear my prayer

	455	Angel voices, ever singing (441)
	120	Lord of beauty, thine the splendour (111)
	294	How glorious Zion's courts appear (299, 537, PP 91)
	407	A fortress sure is God our King (401, 363, **596**)
	583	*Lord, enthroned in heavenly splendour*
	372	Ye servants of God, your Master proclaim (496)
	68	Living under the shadow of his wing

Overseas

I	23	God shall endure for aye; he doth (**312**)		36	The Lord is King! lift up thy voice (**347**)
II	133	Break forth, O living light of God (**333**)		370	When morning gilds the skies
III	497	God of mercy, God of grace (496, 494)		323	'Thy Kingdom come!' – on bended knee (**225, 393**)
IV	500	Christ for the world we sing (505, 476)		**167**	His large and great dominion shall (425, 382, 413)
V	586	*Father, we thank thee who hast planted*		586	*Father, we thank thee who hast planted*
VI	300	At the name of Jesus (657)		374	To God be the glory! great things he hath done
CH	467	Take our gifts, O loving Jesus (501)		427	The Church is wherever God's people are praising (502)
SGP	63	Let the world unite and sing		34	Go tell everyone

All Saints (1st November)

I	534	For all the saints who from their labours rest (**533**)		532	Hark how the adoring hosts above (**5**)
II	119	Enter thy courts, thou Word of life (122)		80	Lord Jesus, think on me (129, **127**)
III	**346**	O Lord, thou art my God and King (363, 372)		606	O Lord of life, where'er they be (437, **531**, PP 145)
IV	473	Lord, who in thy perfect wisdom (**530**, 536, PP 84)		541	The Son of God goes forth to war (538, 286)
V	572	*Come, risen Lord, and deign to be our guest (584)*		582	*In love, from love, thou camest forth, O Lord*
VI	463	Forth in thy Name, O Lord, I go (608)		542	Sing Alleluia forth in duteous praise (640, 543)
SGP	77	Many are the lightbeams		92	Praise the Lord

Remembrance Day

I	**24**	God is our refuge and our strength (**1**, 611)	10	Christ is made the sure foundation (**392**)
II	**531**	Behold what witnesses unseen (538)	87	Be thou my Vision, O Lord of my heart (**24**)
III	**606**	O Lord of life, where'er they be (PP 98)	322	The Lord will come and not be slow (**394**)
IV	**505**	Christ is the world's true light (520, 504)	518	Lord, while for all mankind we pray (517 (1-2 and 5-6))
V	*580*	*And now, O Father, mindful of the love*	**565**	*I'll of salvation take the cup*
VI	**167**	(4-6) His name for ever shall endure (534, 481)	640	Praise ye the Lord, ye servants of the Lord (480)
SGP	62	Lead us, O Father in the paths of peace	30	From creation's start

St Andrew's Day (30th November)

I	**489**	I joy'd when to the house of God (37)	39	Stand up, and bless the Lord
II	115	Come down, O love Divine (129)	**126**	God's perfect law revives the soul (130)
III	211	Jesus calls us! O'er the tumult (PP 85)	476	For my sake and the Gospel's go (**136**)
IV	519	Judge Eternal, throned in splendour (**531**)	520	O God of earth and altar (518)
V	**565**	*I'll of salvation take the cup*	*568*	*Father most loving, listen to thy children*
VI	471	Lift up your heads, ye gates of brass (495)	638	Lord, dismiss us with thy blessing (517 (1-2 and 5-6))
SGP	118	Will you come and follow me	23	Come with me, come wander

Christmas Eve

(1) 193; 170, 174; 176, 186; 181, 171; 192, 178; 191; 169.

(2) 160; 172; 173, 175, 176; 179, 180, 182; 195; 169, 191.

SGP   **(1)** 30 From creation's start

          (2) 89 Oh, the love of my Lord

Three Series of Services for Holy Week

1. Themes for Holy Week

Monday Penitence	Tuesday Obedience	Wednesday Service	Thursday The Institution of the Eucharist and the New Commandment
295 (1-3 and 6)	211	409	667
PP 130	PP 88	PP 42	PP 69 (1-21 and 29-36)
82	682	436	580
95 (1-3)	238	510	589

Friday Morning	Friday Evening The Cross	Saturday
243	240, 243, PP 118 (1-17)	PP 16, 252
PP 40	259	261
83	304	224, 673
301, 254	640	

2. The Events of Holy Week

Monday	Tuesday	Wednesday
The Day of Cleansing	The Day of Teaching	The Day of Preparation
69	80	**65**
208	79	**70**
211	688	379
339	685	680
255	241	PP 102
490	PP 32	
63		

Thursday	Friday	Saturday
The Day of the Agony	The Day of the Cross	The Day of the Grave
666	243	259
83	247	261
237	253	684
565	251	695
242	254	PP 130
238	380	
PP 143	PP 32, PP 40	

3. The Seven Words from the Cross

1. 'Father, forgive them; they do not know what they are doing' (Luke 23:
34)
   25; 69, 82, 216, 666; 244; 439, 680; **63, 66.**

2. 'I tell you this: today you shall be with me in Paradise' (Luke 23:43)
   65; 225, 80; 245; 430, 95, 607, 684; PP 16, PP 143 (1-11).

3. 'Mother, there is your son; . . . there is your mother' (John 19:26f)
   8, 667; 81; 246; 377, 259, 460, 461; PP 63 (1-8).

4. 'My God, my God why hast thou forsaken me?' (Mark 15: 34)
   70; 663, **295**; 247; 377, 695, 397; **239**, PP 88.

5. 'I thirst' (John 19: 28)
   74; 79, 64; 248; 238, 379, 212, 388; **231**, PP 69 (13b-21 and 29-36).

6. 'It is accomplished' (John 19:30)
   241, 242, 243; 83, 251; 249; 380, 252, 257; PP 32, PP 40 (1-10).

7. 'Father, into thy hands I commit my spirit' (Luke 23:46)
   256, 257, 50; 253; 250; 254, 258, **603**, 606; PP 31 (1-8).

SGP The following may be used at appropriate points during Holy Week.

   12 Behold the lamb of God
   42 Here hangs a man discarded
   61 Kyrie eleison
   74 Lord, to whom shall we go
   80 Night has fallen
   85 O Lord, hear my prayer
   99 Stay with me
   114 Were you there

Notes

Notes

Psalms

1　The metrical psalter currently in use in the Church of Scotland is *The Scottish Psalter, 1929, Metrical Version*, which goes back to 1650 for its words and to 1929 for its music. It is still available either as a separate volume or bound together with CH3. An attempt has been made to use as much of the psalter as possible. Numbers in italics within brackets indicate that the psalm may be found in CH3 at that number.

2　Prose psalms may be read or sung. The reading of psalms, or the reciting of psalms to a short melodic formula, has the advantage of allowing the worshippers to use whole psalms or larger portions of psalms than would be convenient if only a metrical version were being used.

3　The reading may be antiphonal, with the psalm being read verse about by two alternating groups; or it may be responsorial, with a verse or phrase of the psalm being used as a refrain and said by the congregation at appropriate points during the reading of the psalm; or it may be in unison, with the whole psalm being read by the whole congregation.

4　*The Scottish Psalter, 1929, Authorized Version, Pointed with Chants,* is still in print; and there is a variety of different styles of chants in CH3.

5　Section One follows the calendar and themes of *The Book of Common Order (1979),* and the adjoining index shows how many of the psalms can be used in this way.

6　It is not necessary to confine the only psalm of the day always to the beginning of the service, and indeed many psalms cannot be used in this way. Section Two follows the structure of CH3 and provides opportunities for the psalms to be used at various points in the service.

7 The letter 'S' indicated psalms which may be sung, usually from the metrical psalter, but occasionally from some other version.

8 The letter 'R' indicates psalms which may be read or chanted. Since the numbering of verses varies from version to version, care should be taken to ensure that any portion selected from any version is a complete unit. Here, the numbering of the Authorized Version is first given, and if it differs, the numbering of *The Psalms: A New Translation for Worship* (Collins) follows in brackets.

SECTION 1
for use with the Lectionary

Ninth Sunday before Christmas
The Creation

S.   **8; 19** 1-6; **19** 7-14 *(125)*
R.   **19; 104; 104** 1-5, 30-34 *(326)*

Eighth Sunday before Christmas
The Fall

S.   **25** 4-10; **51** 1-12 *(64)*; **143** (second version) 6-12
R.   **32; 51** 1-4, 6-12 *(63)*; **53**

Seventh Sunday before Christmas
The Election of God's People: Abraham

S.   **34** 1-10; **139** *(68)*
R.   **105** 1-12; **107** 1-9

Sixth Sunday before Christmas
The Promise of Redemption: Moses

S.   **106** 1-5
R.   **77; 78; 105** 13-45; **106; 114; 136**

121

E

Fifth Sunday before Christmas

The Remnant

S.   **124** (second version) *(392)*; **125; 126**

R.   **74; 79; 124-125-126; 137**

Fourth Sunday before Christmas (Advent I)

The Advent hope

S.   **40** 1-4 *(73)*; **130**

R.   **45; 72; 96-97-98**

Third Sunday before Christmas (Advent II)

The Word of God in the Old Testament

S.   **1; 19** 7-11; **119** 33-40

R.   **19** 7-14; **29; 119**

Second Sunday before Christmas (Advent III)

The Forerunner

S.   **15; 27** 1, 3-5, 14 *(26)*

R.   **27; 141; 142**

First Sunday before Christmas (Advent IV)

The Annunciation

S.   **40** 1-4 *(73)*; **119** 41-48

R.   **45; 113; 131**

Christmas Day

The Birth of Christ

S.   **19** 1-6; **85** 8-13

R.   **110; 132**

First Sunday after Christmas

The Wise Men

S.   **67; 72** 8, 10, 11, 17-19 *(167)*; **145** (second version) 1-7; **148** (second version)

R.   **72** 1, 2, 5, 11, 17-19 *(158)*; **86** 1-10; **96; 138**

Second Sunday after Christmas

(a)   The Presentation in the Temple

S.   **27** 4-6; **84** 1-5; **90** 14-17

R.   **84; 96**

(b)   The Visit to Jerusalem

S.   **65** 1-4; **122**

R.   **27; 63; 116** 12-19

Third Sunday after Christmas

The Baptism of Christ

S.   **36** 5-10

R.   **2; 89** 1-8, 19-29 (19-30); **91**

Fourth Sunday after Christmas

The First Disciples

S.   **67; 105** 1-5; **145** (second version), 1-6, 21

R.   **18** 16-32 (18-34); **67** *(598)*

Fifth Sunday after Christmas

The First Sign

(a)   **The Wedding at Cana**

S.   **89** 15-18

R.   **116** 12-19 (11-18); **128**

(b)   **The New Temple**

S.   **138; 150**

R.   **48; 138; 149-150**

Sixth Sunday after Christmas

(a)   **The Friend of Sinners**

S.   **42** 1-5; **145** (second version) 4-12; **146** 5-10

R.   **14; 42** 1-5, 8-11 (1-7, 10-14) *(231)*; **66; 70**

(b)   **Life for the World**

S.   **16** 7-11; **23** *(387)*; **28** 6-9

R.   **16; 23** *(389)*; **28; 133**

Ninth Sunday before Easter

Christ the Teacher

S.   **103** 8-13; **119** 33-40

R.   **49**

Eighth Sunday before Easter

Christ the Healer

S.   **126; 147** 1-5
R.   **94; 139** 13-18 (12-18)

Seventh Sunday before Easter

Christ, Worker of Miracles

S.   **46** 8-11; **96** 1-5
R.   **46; 115**

Ash Wednesday

S.   **51** 1-12 *(64)*; **130**
R.   **6; 51** 1-4, 6-12 *(63)*

Sixth Sunday before Easter (Lent I)

The King and the Kingdom: Temptation

S.   **51** 1-12 *(64)*; **119** 1-8; **130**
R.   **17; 51; 59**

Fifth Sunday before Easter (Lent II)

The King and the Kingdom: Conflict

S.   **61** 1-4; **119** 49-56
R.   **18** 1-19 (1-21); **64; 120**

Fourth Sunday before Easter (Lent III)

The King and the Kingdom: Suffering

S.   **63** 1-8; **119** 81-88
R.   **38; 73** 1-6, 13-28

Third Sunday before Easter (Lent IV)

The King and the Kingdom: Transfiguration

S.   **34** 1-9; **36** 5-10; **119** 145-152
R.   **34; 35**

Second Sunday before Easter (Passion)

The King and the Kingdom: Victory of the Cross

S.   **119** 105-112; **121**
R.   **22** *(239)*; **42-43; 143**

First Sunday before Easter (Palm)

The Way of the Cross

S.   **24** 7-10; **118** 19-29
R.   **24; 45** 1-7; **69**

Maundy Thursday

S.   **116** 1-7
R.   **116; 140**

Good Friday

S.   **69** 16-21; **143** (second version) 6-12
R.   **40; 42; 42** 1-5, 8-11 *(231)*; **54; 88**

Easter Day

The Resurrection of Christ

S.   **98** 1-4; **118** 19-29

R.   **16** 5-11; **114**

First Sunday after Easter

(a)   **The Upper Room Appearances**

S.   **118** 15-19

R.   **145**

(b)   **The Bread of Life**

S.   **23** *(387)*; **34** 1-10

R.   **107** 1-22

Second Sunday after Easter

(a)   **The Emmaus Road**

S.   **80** 17-19; **111** 1-4; **150**

R.   **111**

(b)   **The Good Shepherd**

S.   **23** *(387)*; **80** 1, 17-19

R.   **3; 23**

Third Sunday after Easter

(a)   **The Lakeside**

S.   **16** 7-11; **20** 1-6

R.   **30**

(b)   **The Resurrection and the Life**

S.   **27** 1, 3-5, 14 *(26)*
R.   **117; 133**

Fourth Sunday after Easter

(a)   **The Charge to Peter**

S.   **89** 15-18
R.   **37** 23-40 (23-41); **87**

(b)   **The Way, the Truth and the Life**

S.   **100; 118** 19-25
R.   **119** 9-32

Fifth Sunday after Easter

Going to the Father

S.   **68** 32-35
R.   **110; 123-124**

Ascension Day

S.   **24** 7-10; **68** 18-20 *(285)*
R.   **47** *(284)*

Sixth Sunday after Easter

The Ascension of Christ

S.   **68** 18-20 *(285)*; **93**
R.   **21** 1-7; **108** 1-6

Pentecost

The Gift of the Spirit

S.   **96** 1-6; **98**

R.   **96; 99; 104** 24-33 (26-35); **104** 1-5, 30-34 *(326)*

First Sunday after Pentecost (Trinity) (St. Columba)

(a)   The Riches of God

S.   **93; 136** (second version) 1-5, 23-26 *(137)*; **147** 1-5

R.   **29; 93; 97; 136** *(350)*

(b)   The Church's Message

S.   **57** 7-11; **102** 16-22

R.   **48**

Second Sunday after Pentecost

(a)   The People of God

S.   **89** 15-18; **116** 13-19

R.   **80; 81** 8-16; **132; 135**

(b)   The Church's Unity and Fellowship

S.   **122; 133**

R.   **5; 78** 1-8; **86**

Third Sunday after Pentecost

(a)   The Life of the Baptised

S.   **28** 6-9; **84** 8-12

R.   **6; 32**

(b)   The Church's Confidence in Christ

S.   **34** 1-9; **118** 19-26

R.   **55; 91**

Fourth Sunday after Pentecost

(a) **The Freedom of the Sons of God**

S.   **63** 1-8; **124** (second version) *(392)*

R.   **31; 144**

(b) **The Church's Mission to the Individual**

S.   **72** 1-7

R.   **57; 109** 21-31 (20-30); **142**

Fifth Sunday after Pentecost

(a) **The New Law**

S.   **19** 7-11; **119** 33-40 *(127)*

R.   **119** 57-64; **119** 89-96

(b) **The Church's Mission to all Men**

S.   **50** 1-6; **66** 1-4, 8-9, 20; **126**

R.   **47; 113**

Sixth Sunday after Pentecost

The New Man

S.   **1; 37** 3-7, 23-24

R.   **26; 101; 112; 141**

Seventh Sunday after Pentecost

The More Excellent Way

S.   **23** *(387)*; **103** 8-13

R.   **62**

Eighth Sunday after Pentecost

The Fruit of the Spirit

S.   **25** 4-10

R.   **27** 1-6 (1-8); **85**

Ninth Sunday after Pentecost

The Whole Armour of God

S.   **61** 1-5; **62** 5-8

R.   **7; 18** 1-6, 30-36 (1-7, 32-38); **44; 76; 83**

Tenth Sunday after Pentecost

The Mind of Christ

S.   **80** 17-19; **86** 8-13

R.   **4; 73** 22-28 (21-28)

Eleventh Sunday after Pentecost

The Serving Community

S.   **72** 1-7; **102** (second version) 16-22

R.   **40** 9-17 (11-22); **129**

Twelfth Sunday after Pentecost

The Witnessing Community

S.   **92** 1-4 *(29)*; **96** 1-6

R.   **97; 134-135**

Thirteenth Sunday after Pentecost

The Suffering Community

S. **43** 3-5 *(7)*; **71** 1-5

R. **10; 11; 12; 30; 39; 60** 1-5, 11-12

Fourteenth Sunday after Pentecost

The Neighbour

S. **15** *(5)*

R. **112**

Fifteenth Sunday after Pentecost

The Family

S. **78** 4b-7 *(547)*

R. **127-128**

Sixteenth Sunday after Pentecost

Those in Authority

S. **89** 11-15; **93** *(140)*

R. **21; 75; 99**

Seventeenth Sunday after Pentecost

The Proof of Faith

S. **34** 8-15

R. **49; 52; 82**

Eighteenth Sunday after Pentecost

The Offering of Life

S.   **20** 1-5; **96** 7-13

R.   **54; 90; 95**

Nineteenth Sunday after Pentecost

The Life of Faith

S.   **103** 1-5 (*351*); **139** (*68*)

R.   **41; 139** 1-12 (1-11)

Twentieth Sunday after Pentecost

Citizens of Heaven

S.   **16** 7-11; **23** (*387*); **103** 19-22

R.   **11; 84; 87**

Twenty-first Sunday after Pentecost

Endurance

S.   **23; 37** 35-40; **121** (*139*)

R.   **13; 56; 57**

Twenty-second Sunday after Pentecost

S.   **24** 1-5; **122**

R.   **97**

Twenty-third Sunday after Pentecost

S.   **146** 5-10

R.   **119** 1-8

Christian Unity

S.   **102** (second version) 13-22 (*333*); **122**

R.   **133-134**

Springtime

S.   **65** 9-13

R.   **104** 1, 10-24 (11-26)

Harvest Festival

S.   **24** 1-5; **67** (*493*); **145** (second version) 9-16

R.   **65; 104** 19-31 (21-33); **147** 7-20

Michaelmas (29th September)

S.   **103** 19-22 (*596*); **148** (second version)

R.   **95**

Overseas

S.   **9** 7-11 (*23*); **67; 126**

R.   **72** 8-19 (8-21); **102** 12-28

All Saints (1st November)

S.   **33** 1-5 (*27*); **34** 1-9; **145** (second version) 8-14

R.   **1; 15** (*5*); **100**

Remembrance Day

S.   **124** (second version) (*392*)

R.   **46; 20**

St. Andrew's Day (30th November)

S.   **50** 1-5

R.   **40** 1-11; **87**

INDEX OF PSALMS
used in Section 1

Psalm

52 Pentecost 17
53 8th before Christmas
54 Pentecost 18
55 Pentecost 3b
56 Pentecost 21
57 Pentecost 1b; Pentecost 4b;
   Pentecost 20
58 –
59 Lent 1
60 Pentecost 13
61 Pentecost 9
62 Pentecost 7; Pentecost 9
63 Christmas 2b; Lent 3
64 Lent 2
65 Christmas 2b; Springtime;
   Harvest
66 Christmas 6a; Pentecost 5b
67 Christmas 1; Christmas 4;
   Harvest; Overseas
68 Ascension Day; Easter 6
69 Pentecost 13
70 Christmas 6a
71 Pentecost 13
72 Christmas 1; Advent 1;
   Pentecost 11; Overseas
73 Lent 3; Pentecost 10
74 5th before Christmas
75 Pentecost 16
76 Pentecost 9
77 6th before Christmas
78 6th before Christmas;
   Pentecost 2b; Pentecost 15
79 5th before Christmas
80 Easter 2a; Pentecost 10
81 Pentecost 2a
82 Pentecost 17
83 Pentecost 9
84 Christmas 2a; Pentecost 3a
85 Christmas Day; Pentecost 8

Psalm

86 Christmas 1; Pentecost 2b;
   Pentecost 10
87 Easter 4a; Pentecost 20
88 Good Friday
89 Christmas 3; Pentecost 2a;
   Pentecost 16
90 Christmas 2a; Pentecost 18
91 Christmas 3a; Pentecost 3b
92 Pentecost 12
93 Easter 6; Pentecost 1;
   Pentecost 16
94 8th before Easter
95 Pentecost 18
96 Advent 1; Christmas 1;
   Christmas 2a; Pentecost;
   Pentecost 12; Pentecost 18
97 Advent 1; Pentecost 1;
   Pentecost 12; Pentecost 22
98 Advent 1; Easter Day;
   Pentecost
99 Pentecost; Pentecost 16
100 All Saints
101 Pentecost 6
102 Pentecost 1b; Pentecost 11;
    Christian Unity; Overseas
103 9th before Easter; Pentecost;
    Pentecost 7; Pentecost 19;
    Michaelmas
104 9th before Christmas;
    Pentecost; Springtime;
    Harvest
105 7th before Christmas; 6th
    before Christmas; Christmas
    4
106 6th before Christmas
107 7th before Christmas; Easter
    1b
108 Easter 6 (Ascension)
109 Pentecost 4b

Psalm

110 Christmas Day
111 Easter 2
112 Pentecost 6; Pentecost 14
113 Advent 4; Pentecost 5b
114 6th before Christmas; Easter Day
115 7th before Easter
116 Christmas 2b; Christmas 5a; Maundy Thursday; Pentecost 2a
117 Easter 3b
118 1st before Easter (Palm); Easter Day; Pentecost 3b
119 Advent 2
119 v.1–8. Lent 1; Pentecost 23
v.9–32. Easter 4b
v. 33-40. Advent 2; Pentecost 5a; 9th before Easter
v. 41-48. Advent 4
v. 49-56. Lent 2
v. 57-64. Pentecost 5a
v. 81-88. Lent 3
v. 89-96. Pentecost 5a
v. 105-112. 2nd before Easter (Passion)
v. 145-152. Lent 4
120 Lent 2
121 2nd before Easter (Passion); Pentecost 21
122 Christmas 2b; Pentecost 2b; Pentecost 22; Christian Unity
123 Easter 5
124 5th before Christmas; Easter 5; Pentecost 4a; Remembrance Day

Psalm

125 5th before Christmas
126 5th before Christmas; 8th before Easter; Pentecost 5b; Overseas
127 Pentecost 15
128 Christmas 5a; Pentecost 15
129 Pentecost 11
130 Advent 1; Ash Wednesday; Lent 1
131 Advent 4
132 Christmas Day; Pentecost 2a
133 Christmas 6b; Pentecost 2b; Christian Unity
134 Pentecost 12; Christian Unity
135 Pentecost 12
136 6th before Christmas; Pentecost 1 (Trinity)a
137 5th before Christmas
138 Christmas 1; Christmas 5b
139 7th before Christmas; Pentecost 19
140 Maundy Thursday
141 Advent 3; Pentecost 6
142 Advent 3; Pentecost 4b
143 8th before Christmas; 2nd before Easter (Passion)
144 Pentecost 4a
145 Christmas 1; Christmas 4; Easter 1; Harvest; All Saints
146 Christmas 6a
147 Pentecost 1a; Harvest
148 Christmas 1; Michaelmas
149 Christmas 5b
150 Christmas 5b; Easter 1a

SECTION 2
for use at various points in the Order of Public Worship

Assembling

Approach

S.   **15** (*5*); **23** (*387*);**26** 6-8(*564*); **36** 5-9 (*6*); **42** 1-5; **43** 3-5 (*7*); **65** 1-4 (*28*); **84** 1-5 (*4*); **84** 8-12; **100** (*1*); **102** (second version) 13-18 (*333*); **116** 1-7 (*8*); **122**; **122** 1, 2, 6-9 (*489*)

R.   **23** (*389*); **27** 1-6 (1-8); **27** 7-8 (9-10); **42** 1-5, 8-11 (*231*); **48**; **84**; **132**

Adoration

S.   **8**; **8** 1, 3-5 (*138*); **9** 7-11 (*23*); **27** 1, 3-5, 14 (*26*); **33** 1-5 (*27*); **46** 1-5 (*24*); **50** 1-6; **62** 5-8 (*25*); **93** (*140*); **95** 1-6 (*19*); **96** 1, 2, 6-8 (*22*); **98** 1-3, 5-9 (*348*); **103** 19-22 (*596*); **136** (second version) 1-5, 23-26 (*137*); **145** (second version) 1-6 (*346*); **150** (*138*)

R.   **50** 1-6, 14-23 (*310*); **68** 32-35; **86** 8-17; **89** 1-14; **95** 1-7(*20, 21*); **97**; **98** (*349*); **104** 1-5, 33-34 (*326*); **136** (*350*)

Morning

S.   **57** 5, 7-11; **63** 1-4 (*41*); **92** 1-4 (*29*); **143** (second version) 6-8; **145** (second version) 1-6 (*346*)

R.   **5** 1-8 (1-7); **130** (*66*); **130** (*67*)

Evening

S.   **121** (*139*); **139** 7-14

R.   **4**; **31** 1-8; **91**; **134**; **139** 1-14 (1-13)

Confession

S.   **25** 8-12; **32** 1-2, 5-7; **51** 1-12 (*64*); **130** 1-6a, 7b, 8 (*65*); **139** (*68*)

R.   **32; 51** 1-4, 6-12 (*63*); **86** 3-7

Supplication

S.   **20** 1-5; **25** 4, 5a, 6-10 (*74*); **28** 6-9; **34** 1-9; **34** 1-2, 7-9, 11, 14, 15 (*391*); **40** 1-4 (*73*); **61** 1-4 (*71*); **85** 1, 2, 5-7 (*75*); **116** 1-7 (*8*); **143** (second version) 1, 6-8 (*70*)

R.   **28; 31** 1-5; **31** 15-24 (*17-27*); **85; 116** 1-9

Invocation

S.   **18** 1-7; **27** 9-12; **70** 4-6; **90** 1, 2, 14, 16, 17 (*102*); **106** 1-5, 48 (*101*); **119** 169-176

R.   **17** 6-8

Illumination

S.   **36** 5-9 (*6*); **43** 3-5 (*7*); **119** 33-40 (*127*)

R.   **13; 119** 129-136; **119** 169-176

Holy Scripture

S.   **19** 7-10, 14 (*125*); **19** 7-14 (*126*); **50** (second version) 1-6; **119** 33-40 (*127*)

R.   **50** 1-6, 14, 23 (*310*); **119** 129-136; **138**

Before the Sermon

S.   **46** 7-11

R.   **46** 7-11; **85** 7-8

Intercession

S.   **28** 6-9; **67** (*493*); **84** 8-12; **106** 1-5, 48 (*101*); **122** 1-2, 6-9 (*489*); **147** 1-5 (*136*)

R.   **20** 1-9; **67** (*598*); **86** 6-13; **122**

Commemoration

S.   **16** 7-11; **23** (*387*); **33** 18-22; **80** 17-19; **103** 1-5 (*351*)
R.   **16; 23** (*389*); **33** 12-22 (12-21); **73** 24-28; **84; 87**

Offertory

S.   **96** 1-2, 6-8 (*22*); **116** 13-19; **116** 13-14, 17-19 (*565*)
R.   **51** 15-18; **66** 13-14 (12-13); **76** 11; **107** 21-22

Thanksgiving

S.   **34** 1-9; **92** 1-4 (*29*); **95** 1-6 (*19*); **98** 1-4; **98** 1-3, 5-9 (*348*); **100** (*1*); **103** 1-5 (*351*); **106** 1-5, 48 (*101*); **136** (second version) 1-5, 23-26 (*137*); **145** (second version) 1-6 (*346*); **147** 1-5 (*136*); **148** (second version) (*135*)
R.   **34** 1-10; **95** 1-7 (*20, 21*); **98; 100** (*3*); **104; 105** 1-7; **107** 1-9; **111; 136** (*350*); **138; 145; 147** 1-7

Self-dedication

S.   **84** 8-12; **116** 13-19; **116** 13-14, 17-19 (*565*)
R.   **116** 12-19 (11-18)

Dismissal

S.   **72** 17-19; **103** 19-22 (*596*)
R.   **57** 5, 7-11; **103** 17-22; **106** 48 (*50*); **117**

Evening

S.   **121** (*139*)
R.   **4** 8; **31** 5; **134**

Notes

Lectionary and Collects

A TABLE OF LESSONS FROM
HOLY SCRIPTURE FOR TWO YEARS

THIS LECTIONARY is that prepared by the Joint Liturgical Group and published in 1967 in *The Calendar and Lectionary: A Reconsideration,* with some minor modifications.

Bold type denotes the 'controlling lesson' for each day: the significance of this is explained in *The Calendar and Lectionary*; see especially p 18: 'In the pre-Christmas period, the Old Testament should provide the controlling lection. In the post-Pentecost period, the Acts and the Epistles should provide the controlling lection. From Christmas to Pentecost, the Gospel should control.' If only two of the three readings are used at one service, 'it is greatly to be hoped that the Controlling Lection should always be one of them' (Introduction, p xi).

144

SUNDAYS, etc	FIRST YEAR	SECOND YEAR
9 before Christmas	**Gen.** 1. 1-3, 24-31a Col. 1. 15-20 John 1. 1-14	**Gen.** 2. 4b-9, 15-25 Rev. 4. 1-11 John 3. 1-18
8 before Christmas	**Gen.** 3. 1-15 Rom. 7. 7-12 John 3. 13-21	**Gen.** 4. 1-10 1 John 3. 9-18 Mark 7. 14-23
7 before Christmas	**Gen.** 12. 1-9 Rom. 4. 13-25 John 8. 51-58	**Gen.** 22. 1-18 Jas. 2. 14-24 Luke 20. 9-16
6 before Christmas	**Exod.** 3. 1-15 Heb. 3. 1-6 John 6. 27-35	**Exod.** 6. 2-8 Heb. 11. 17-29 Mark 13. 5-13
5 before Christmas	**1 Kgs.** 19. 9-18 Rom. 11. 13-24 Matt. 24. 38-44	**Isa.** 10. 20-23 Rom. 9. 19-29 Mark 13. 14-23
Advent 1 (4 before Christmas)	**Isa.** 52. 1-10 1 Thess. 5. 1-11 Luke 21. 25-33	**Isa.** 51. 4-11 Rom. 13. 8-14 Matt. 25. 31-46
Advent 2 (3 before Christmas)	**Isa.** 55. 1-11 Rom. 15. 4-13 John 5. 36-47	**Isa.** 64. 1-5 2 Tim. 3. 14-4. 5 Luke 4. 14 21
Advent 3 (2 before Christmas)	**Isa.** 40. 1-11 1 Cor. 4. 1-5 John 1. 19-27	**Mal.** 3. 1-5 Phil. 4. 4-9 Matt. 11. 2-15
Advent 4 (1 before Christmas)	**Isa.** 11. 1-9 1 Cor. 1. 26-31 Luke 1. 26-38	**Zech.** 2. 10-13 Rev. 21. 1-7 Matt. 1. 18-23
Christmas Day (i)	Mic. 5. 2-4 Titus 2. 11-15 **Luke** 2. 1-20	Mic. 5. 2-4 Titus 2. 11-15 **Luke** 2. 1-20
(ii)	Isa. 9. 2-7 1 John 4. 7-14 **John** 1. 1-14	Isa. 9. 2-7 1 John 4. 7-14 **John** 1. 1-14

145

SUNDAYS, etc	FIRST YEAR	SECOND YEAR
Christmas 1	Isa. 60. 1-6 Heb. 1. 1-4 **Matt.** 2. 1-12	Isa. 49. 7-13 Eph. 3. 1-6 **Matt.** 2. 1-12
Christmas 2	1 Sam. 1. 20-28 Rom. 12. 1-8 **Luke** 2. 21-40	Deut. 16. 1-6 Rom. 8. 12-17 **Luke** 2. 41-52
Christmas 3	1 Sam. 16. 1-13 Acts 10. 34-48 **Matt.** 3. 13-17	Isa. 42. 1-7 Eph. 2. 1-10 **John** 1. 29-34
Christmas 4	Jer. 1. 4-10 Acts 26. 1, 9-18 **Mark** 1. 14-20	1 Sam. 3. 1-10 Gal. 1. 11-24 **John** 1. 35-51
Christmas 5	Exod. 33. 12-23 1 John 1. 1-4 **John** 2. 1-11	1 Kgs. 8. 22-30 1 Cor. 3. 10-17 **John** 2. 13-22
Christmas 6	Hos. 14. 1-7 Philem. 1-16 **Mark** 2. 13-17	1 Kgs. 10. 1-13 Eph. 3. 8-19 **John** 4. 7-14
9 before Easter	Isa. 30. 18-21 1 Cor. 4. 8-13 **Matt.** 5. 1-12	Prov. 3. 1-8 1 Cor. 2. 1-10 **Luke** 8. 4-15
8 before Easter	Zeph. 3. 14-20 Jas. 5. 13-16 **Mark** 2. 1-12	2 Kgs. 5. 1-14 2 Cor. 12. 1-10 **Mark** 1. 35-45
7 before Easter	Deut. 8. 1-6 Phil. 4. 10-20 **John** 6. 1-14	Jonah 1. 1-17 Jas. 1. 2-12 **Mark** 4. 35-41
Ash Wednesday	Isa. 58. 1-8 1 Cor. 9. 24-27 **Matt.** 6. 16-21	Amos 5. 6-15 Jas. 4. 1-8a **Luke** 18. 9-14
Lent 1 (6 before Easter)	Deut. 30. 15-20 Heb. 2. 14-18 **Matt.** 4. 1-17	Deut. 6. 10-17 Heb. 4. 12-16 **Luke** 4. 1-13

SUNDAYS, etc		FIRST YEAR	SECOND YEAR
Lent 2 (5 before Easter)		2 Kgs. 6. 8-17 1 John 4. 1-6 **Luke** 11. 14-26	Isa. 35. 1-10 1 John 3. 1-8 **Matt.** 12. 22-32
Lent 3 (4 before Easter)		Isa. 59. 12-20 1 Pet. 2. 19-25 **Matt.** 16. 13-28	Isa. 45. 18-25 Col. 1. 24-29 **Luke** 9. 18-27
Lent 4 (3 before Easter)		Exod. 34. 29-35 2 Cor. 3. 12-18 **Matt.** 17. 1-8	1 Kgs. 19. 1-12 2 Pet. 1. 16-19 **Luke** 9. 28-36
Passion Sunday (2 before Easter)		Isa. 63. 1-9 Col. 2. 8-15 **John** 12. 20-32	Jer. 31. 31-34 Heb. 9. 11-15 **Mark** 10. 32-45
Palm Sunday (1 before Easter)		Zech. 9. 9-12 1 Cor. 1. 18-25 **Mark** 11. 1-11 (or **Matt.** 26 and 27. 1-61)	Isa. 52. 13 53. 12 Heb. 10. 1-10 **Matt.** 21. 1-11 (or **Matt.** 26 and 27. 1-61)
Good Friday		Exod. 12. 1-11 Heb. 10. 11-25 **John** (18 and) 19. 1-37	Exod. 12. 1-11 Heb. 10. 11-25 **John** (18 and) 19. 1-37
Easter Day	(i)	Isa. 12. 1-6 Rev. 1. 12-18 **Mark** 16. 1-8	Isa. 12. 1-6 1 Cor. 5. 7b-8 **Matt.** 28. 1-10
	(ii)	Exod. 14. 15-22 1 Cor. 15. 12-20 **John** 20. 1-18	Exod. 14. 15-22 1 Cor. 15. 12-20 **John** 20. 1-18
Easter 1		Exod. 15. 1-11 1 Pet. 1. 3-9 **John** 20. 19-29	Exod. 16. 4-15 1 Cor. 15. 53-58 **John** 6. 25-40
Easter 2		Isa. 25. 6-9 Rev. 19. 6-9 **Luke** 24. 13-35	Ezek. 34. 7-15 1 Pet. 5. 1-11 **John** 10. 7-18

SUNDAYS, etc	FIRST YEAR	SECOND YEAR
Easter 3	Isa. 61. 1-3 1 Cor. 15. 1-11 **John** 21. 1-14	1 Kgs. 17. 17-24 Col. 3. 1-11 **John** 11. 17-27
Easter 4	Isa. 62. 1-5 Rev. 3. 14-22 **John** 21. 15-22	Prov. 4. 10-18 2 Cor. 4. 11-18 **John** 14. 1-11
Easter 5	Isa. 51. 1-6 1 Cor. 15. 21-28 **John** 16. 25-33	Deut. 34. 1-12 Rom. 8. 28-39 **John** 16. 12-24
Ascension Day	Dan. 7. 13-14 Acts 1. 1-11 **Matt.** 28. 16-20	Dan. 7. 13-14 Acts 1. 1-11 **Matt.** 28. 16-20
Easter 6	Dan. 7. 9-14 Eph. 1. 15-23 **Luke** 24. 44-53	2 Kgs. 2. 1-15 Eph. 4. 1-8, 11-13 **Luke** 24. 44-53
Pentecost	Joel 2. 23-29 **Acts** 2. 1-11 John 14. 15-27	Joel 2. 28-32 **Acts** 2. 1-11 John 14. 15-27
Pentecost 1 (Trinity Sunday)	Isa. 6. 1-8 **Eph.** 1. 3-14 John 14. 8-17	Deut. 6. 4-9 **Acts** 2. 22-4, 32-6 Matt. 11. 25-30
Pentecost 2	Exod. 19. 1-6 **1 Pet.** 2. 1-10 John 15. 1-5	2 Sam. 7. 4-16 **Acts** 2. 37-47 Luke 14. 15-24
Pentecost 3	Deut. 6. 17-25 **Rom.** 6. 1-11 John 15. 6-11	Deut. 8. 11-20 **Acts** 4. 5-12 Luke 8. 41-55
Pentecost 4	Deut. 7. 6-9a **Gal.** 3. 23-4. 7 John 15. 12-15	Josh. 24. 14-25 **Acts** 8. 26-38 Luke 15. 1-10
Pentecost 5	Exod. 20. 1-17 **Eph.** 5. 1-10 Matt. 19. 16-26	Ruth 1. 8-17, 22 **Acts** 11. 4-18 Luke 17. 11-19

SUNDAYS, etc	FIRST YEAR	SECOND YEAR
Pentecost 6	Exod. 24. 3-8 **Col.** 3. 12-17 Luke 15. 11-32	Mic. 6. 1-8 **Eph.** 4. 17-32 Mark 10. 46-52
Pentecost 7	Hos. 11. 1-9 **1 Cor.** 13. 1-13 Matt. 18. 21-35	Deut. 10. 12 11. 1 **Rom.** 8. 1-11 Mark 12. 28-34
Pentecost 8	Ezek. 36. 24-28 **Gal.** 5. 16-25 John 15. 16-27	Ezek. 37. 1-14 **1 Cor.** 12. 4-13 Luke 6. 27-38
Pentecost 9	Josh. 1. 1-9 **Eph.** 6. 10-18a John 17. 11-19	1 Sam. 17. 37-50 **2 Cor.** 6. 1-10 Mark 9. 14-29
Pentecost 10	Job 42. 1-6 **Phil.** 2. 1-13 John 13. 1-15	1 Sam. 24. 9-17 **Gal.** 6. 1-10 Luke 7. 36-50
Pentecost 11	Isa. 42. 1-7 **2 Cor.** 4. 1-10 John 13. 33-36	1 Chr. 29. 1-9 **Phil.** 1. 1-11 Luke 17. 5-10
Pentecost 12	Isa. 49. 1-6 **2 Cor.** 5. 14-21 John 17. 20-26	Mic. 4. 1-7 **Acts** 17. 22-31 Matt. 5. 13-16
Pentecost 13	Isa. 50. 4-9 **1 Pet.** 4. 12-19 John 16. 1-11	Jer. 12. 1-6 **Acts** 20. 17-35 Matt. 10. 16-22
Pentecost 14	Lev. 19. 9-18 **Rom.** 12. 9-21 Luke 10. 25-37	Deut. 15. 7-11 **1 John** 4. 15-21 Luke 16. 19-31
Pentecost 15	Isa. 54. 1-8 **Eph.** 5. 21 6. 4 Mark 10. 2 16	Gen. 45. 1-15 **1 Pet.** 3. 1-9 Luke 14 25-33
Pentecost 16	Isa. 45. 1-7 **Rom.** 13. 1-7 Matt. 22. 15-22	1 Kgs. 3. 5-15 **1 Tim.** 2. 1-7 Luke 11. 1-13

SUNDAYS, etc	FIRST YEAR	SECOND YEAR
Pentecost 17	Jer. 7. 1-7 **Jas.** 1. 22-27 Matt. 7. 21-29	Jer. 32. 6-15 **Gal.** 2. 20 3-9 Luke 7. 1-10
Pentecost 18	Deut. 26. 1-11 **2 Cor.** 8. 1-9 Matt. 5. 21-26	Eccles. 38. 24-34 (or Neh. 6. 1-16) **1 Pet.** 4. 7-11 Matt. 25. 14-29
Pentecost 19	Gen. 28. 10-22 **Heb.** 11. 1-3, 7-16 Luke 5. 1-11	Dan. 6. 10-23 **Rom.** 5. 1-11 Luke 19. 1-10
Pentecost 20	Jer. 29. 1, 4-14 **Phil.** 3. 7-21 John 17. 1-10	Isa. 33. 17-22 **Rev.** 7. 9-17 Matt. 25. 1-13
Pentecost 21	Dan. 3. 13-25 **Heb.** 11. 32 12. 2 Luke 9. 51-62	Gen. 32. 24-30 **1 Cor.** 9. 19-27 Matt. 7. 13-20

EXTRA SUNDAYS AFTER CHRISTMAS
(if needed before Easter is fixed)

Christmas 7	Joel 2. 15-22 2 Cor. 3. 14-11 **Mark** 2. 18-22
Christmas 8	Isa. 1. 10-17 1 Cor. 3. 18-23 **Mark** 2. 23 3.6

EXTRA SUNDAYS AFTER PENTECOST
(if needed before Easter is fixed)

Pentecost 22	Exod. 19. 16-24 **Heb.** 12. 18-29 John 4. 19-26
Pentecost 23	Lam. 3. 19-26 **1 Thess.** 5. 12-24 Matt. 20. 1-15

LESSONS FOR SPECIAL DAYS

Lessons are provided here, and collects on p. 175 for the same additional occasions for which lists of hymns are provided in *The Year's Praise*.

SUNDAYS, etc	FIRST YEAR	SECOND YEAR
Christian Unity	Ezek. 37. 15-24 1 Cor. 3. 1-11 Matt. 28. 16-20	Jer. 33. 6-9 Eph. 4. 1-6 John 17. 11b-23
Springtime	Gen. 8. 15-22 Gal. 6. 7-10 Matt. 6. 24-30	Song of S. 2. 8-13 2 Cor. 9. 6-15 John 12. 20-26
Harvest Festival	Deut. 26. 1-11 Rev. 14. 14-18 Matt. 13. 24-33	Deut. 8. 1-10 Acts 14. 13-17 Luke 12. 13-21
Michaelmas (29th September)	2 Kings 6. 8-17 Rev. 12. 7-12a Matt. 18. 1-6, 10	
Overseas	1 Chr. 16. 8-24 Rom. 1. 8-17 Luke 10. 1-11, 17-20	Isa. 43. 5-13 Acts 16. 1-15 Matt. 8. 5-13
All Saints (1st November)	Jer. 31. 31-34 Heb. 12. 18-24 Matt. 5. 1-12	Dan. 7. 27 Rev. 7. 9-17 Matt. 5. 1-12
Remembrance Day	Isa. 25. 1-9 Rom. 8. 31-35 John 15. 9-17	Deut. 4. 9-14 Rev. 22. 1-5 Matt. 5. 38-48
St. Andrew's Day (30th November)	Isa. 49. 1-12 Phil. 1. 3-11 John 1. 35-42	Zech. 8. 20-23 Rom. 10. 12-15 Matt. 4. 12-20

THE COLLECTS

9 before Christmas

Almighty God,
you have created the heavens and the earth
and made man in your own image.
Teach us to discern your hand in all your works
and to serve you with reverence and thanksgiving;
through Jesus Christ our Lord,
who with you and the Holy Spirit reigns supreme
over all things now and for ever.

JLG

8 before Christmas

Almighty God,
you have given your Son Jesus Christ
    to break the power of evil.
Free us from all that darkens and ensnares us
and bring us to eternal light and joy;
through the power of him
who is alive and reigns with you and the Holy Spirit,
one God, now and for ever.

JLG

7 before Christmas

Almighty God,
your chosen servant Abraham
faithfully obeyed your call
and rejoiced in your promise
that, in him, all the families of the earth should be blessed.
Give us a faith like his,
that, in us, your promises may be fulfilled;
through Jesus Christ our Lord.   *JLG*

6 before Christmas

Lord God our redeemer,
who heard the cry of your people
and sent your servant Moses to lead them our of slavery:
free us from the tyranny of sin and death
and, by the leading of your Spirit,
bring us to our promised land;
through Jesus Christ our Lord.

CSI, Pentecost 22 (adapted)

5 before Christmas

1   Almighty God,
who spoke to the prophets
that they might make your will and purpose known:
inspire the guardians of your truth,
that the many may be blessed through the few
and the children of earth be made one
        with the saints in glory;
by the power of Jesus Christ our Lord,
who alone redeemed mankind
and reigns with you and the Holy Spirit,
one God, now and for ever.

Alternative Services, Series 3, Collects

2   Stir up, O Lord,
the wills of your faithful people;
that richly bearing the fruit of good works,
they may by you be richly rewarded;
through Jesus Christ our Lord.

BCP, Trinity 25 (adapted)

Advent 1 (4 before Christmas)

Almighty God,
give us grace to cast away the works of darkness
and to put on the armour of light
now in the time of this mortal life,
in which your Son Jesus Christ
    came to us in great humility:
so that on the last day,
when he shall come again in his glorious majesty
    to judge the living and the dead,
we may rise to the life immortal;
through him who is alive and reigns
    with you and the Holy Spirit,
one God, now and for ever.

BCP, Advent 1 (adapted)

Advent 2 (3 before Christmas)

Eternal God,
who caused all holy scriptures
    to be written for our learning:
help us to hear them,
to read, mark, learn, and inwardly digest them
that, through patience, and the comfort of your holy word,
we may embrace and for ever hold fast
    the hope of everlasting life.
which you have given us in our Saviour Jesus Christ.

BCP Advent (adapted)

Advent 3 (2 before Christmas)

Almighty God,
who sent your servant John the Baptist
to prepare your people for the coming of your Son:
inspire the ministers and stewards of your truth
to turn our disobedient hearts to the law of love;

F

that when he comes again in glory,
we may stand with confidence before him as our judge;
who is alive and reigns with you and the Holy Spirit,
one God, now and for ever.

JLG

Advent 4 (1 before Christmas).

Heavenly Father,
who chose the Virgin Mary, full of grace,
to be the mother of our Lord and Saviour:
fill us with your grace,
that in all things we may accept your holy will
and with her rejoice in your salvation;
through Jesus Christ our Lord.

JLG

Christmas Day

1   Eternal God,
     who made this most holy night
     to shine with the brightness of your one true light:
     bring us who have known the revelation
             of that light on earth,
     to see the radiance of your heavenly glory;
     through Jesus Christ our Lord.

JLG

2   All praise to you,
             Almighty God and heavenly king,
     who sent your Son into the world
     to take our nature upon him
     and to be born of a pure virgin:
     grant that, as we are born again in him,

so he may continually dwell in us
and reign on earth as he reigns in heaven
with you and the Holy Spirit
now and for ever.

JLG

3   Almighty God,
     who wonderfully created us in your own image
     and yet more wonderfully restored us
     through your Son Jesus Christ:
     grant that, as he came to share in our humanity,
     so we may share the life of his divinity;
     who is alive and reigns with you and the Holy Spirit,
     one God, now and for ever.

JLG

Christmas 1

Eternal God,
who by the shining of a star
led the wise men to the worship of your Son:
guide by your light the nations of the earth,
that the whole world may behold your glory;
through Jesus Christ our Lord.

CSI, Christmas 2 (adapted)

Christmas 2

1   Almighty Father,
     whose Son Jesus Christ
          was presented in the Temple
     and acclaimed the light of the nations:
     grant that in him we may be presented before you
     and through him may bring light to the world;
     through Jesus Christ our Lord.

JLG

2   O God,
             your blessed son Jesus came into the world
                 to do your will.
         Grant that we may ever have
             the pattern of his life before our eyes
             and find it our delight to do your will
                 and to finish your work;
         through the same Jesus Christ our Lord.
                       Colquhoun, Parish Prayers, 321 (adapted)

Christmas 3

         Almighty God,
         who anointed Jesus at his baptism with the Holy Spirit
         and declared him to be your Son:
         send your Holy Spirit upon us
             who have been baptized in his name,
         that we may surrender our lives to your service
         and rejoice to be called the children of God;
         through Jesus Christ our Lord

                                                              JLG

Christmas 4

         Almighty God,
         by whose grace alone we are accepted
             and called to your service:
         strengthen us by your Holy Spirit
         and make us worthy of our calling;
         through Jesus Christ our Lord.

                                                              JLG

Christmas 5

         Almighty God,
         in Christ you make all things new.
         Transform the poverty of our nature

by the riches of your grace,
and in the renewal of our lives
make known your heavenly glory;
through Jesus Christ our Lord.

CSI, Christmas 6 (adapted)

Christmas 6

Merciful Lord,
grant to your faithful people
    pardon and peace:
that we may be cleansed from all our sins
and serve you with a quiet mind;
through Jesus Christ our Lord.

BCP, Trinity 21 (adapted)

Christmas 7

Give us, Lord, we pray,
the spirit to think and to do always
    those things that are right:
that we who can do no good things without you
may have power to live
    according to your holy will;
through Jesus Christ our Lord.

BCP, Trinity 9 (adapted)

Christmas 8

Heavenly Father,
whose blessed Son was revealed
    that he might destroy the works of the devil
and make us the children of God
and heirs of eternal life:

grant that we, having this hope,
may purify ourselves even as he is pure;
that when he shall appear in power and great glory
we may be made like him in his eternal and
    glorious kingdom;
where he is alive and reigns with you and the Holy Spirit,
one God, now and for ever.

BCP, Epiphany 6 (adapted)

9 before Easter

Eternal God,
whose Son Jesus Christ is for all
    the way, the truth, and the life:
teach us to walk in his way,
to rejoice in his truth, and to share his risen life;
who is alive and reigns with you and the Holy Spirit,
one God, now and for ever.

JLG (adapted)

8 before Easter

Almighty and everliving God,
whose Son Jesus Christ healed the sick
    and restored them to wholeness of life:
look with compassion on the anguish of the world,
and by your healing power
make whole all peoples and nations;
through our Lord and Saviour Jesus Christ
who is alive and reigns with you and the Holy Spirit,
one God, now and for ever.

JLG (adapted)

7 before Easter

Almighty God,
whose Son Jesus Christ fed the hungry
        with the bread of the Kingdom
        and the word of his mouth:
renew your people with your heavenly grace;
and in all our weakness
sustain us by your true and living bread:
through Jesus Christ our Lord.

JLG

Ash Wednesday

Almighty and everlasting God,
you hate nothing that you have made
and forgive the sins of all those who are penitent.
Create and make in us new and contrite hearts,
that, lamenting our sins and acknowledging our
        wretchedness,
we may receive from you, the God of all mercy,
perfect forgiveness and peace;
through Jesus Christ our Lord.

BCP (adapted)

Lent 1 (6 before Easter)

Almighty God,
whose Son Jesus Christ fasted forty days
        in the wilderness,
and was tempted as we are,
        yet without sin:
give us grace to discipline ourselves
        in submission to your Spirit;
and, as you know our weakness,

so may we know your power to save;
through Jesus Christ our Lord.

JLG

Lent 2 (5 before Easter)

Lord God Almighty,
whose Son Jesus Christ prayed for his disciples
that in all the conflicts of the world
    you would keep them from the evil one:
strengthen us to resist every assault and temptation,
    and to follow you, the only God;
through Jesus Christ our Lord.

JLG

Lent 3 (4 before Easter)

Almighty God,
whose most dear Son went not up to joy
    but first he suffered pain,
and entered not into glory
    before he was crucified:
grant that we, walking in the way of the cross,
may find it to be the way of life and peace;
through Jesus Christ our Lord.

American Prayer Book,
Monday before Easter (adapted)

Lent 4 (3 before Easter)

Almighty Father,
whose Son was revealed in majesty
    before he suffered death upon the cross:
give us faith to perceive his glory,

that we may be strengthened to suffer with him
and be changed into his likeness,
    from glory to glory;
who is alive and reigns with you and the Holy Spirit,
one God, now and forever.

1928 Prayer Book (adapted)

Passion Sunday (2 before Easter)

Most merciful God,
who by the death and resurrection
    of your Son Jesus Christ
delivered and redeemed the world:
grant that by faith in him
    who suffered on the cross,
we may triumph in the power of his victory;
through Jesus Christ our Lord.

JLG

Palm Sunday (1 before Easter)

Almighty and everlasting God,
who in your tender love towards the human race
    sent your Son our Saviour Jesus Christ
to take upon him our flesh
and to suffer death upon the cross,
that all people should follow the example of his
    great humility:
grant that we may both follow the example of his passion
and also be made partakers of his resurrection;
through Jesus Christ our Lord.

BCP (adapted)

Maundy Thursday

1   Almighty and heavenly Father,
     we thank you that

in this wonderful sacrament
you have given us the memorial
 of the passion of your Son Jesus Christ.
Grant us so to reverence
the sacred mysteries of his body and blood,
that our lives may bear abundantly
 the fruits of his redemption;
who is alive and reigns with you and the Holy Spirit,
one God, now and for ever.

1928 Prayer Book, Thanksgiving for the
Institution of Holy Communion (adapted)

2 Almighty Father,
whose Son Jesus Christ has taught us
that what we do for the least of our brethren
 we do also for him:
give us the will to be the servant of others
 as he was the servant of all,
who gave up his life and died for us,
yet is alive and reigns with you and the Holy Spirit,
one God, now and for ever.

JLG

Good Friday

1 Almighty Father,
look with mercy on this your family
for which our Lord Jesus Christ
 was content to be betrayed
 and given up into the hands of wicked men
 and to suffer death upon the cross;
who is alive and glorified
with you and the Holy Spirit,
one God, now and for ever.

BCP (adapted)

2 Almighty and everlasting God,
by whose Spirit the whole body of your faithful
people is governed and sanctified:
hear our prayer which we offer for all members
of your holy Church;
that each in his vocation and ministry
may serve you in holiness and truth
to the glory of your name;
through our Lord and Saviour Jesus Christ.
BCP (adapted)

3 Almighty God,
who called your Church to witness
that you were in Christ
reconciling the world to yourself:
help us to proclaim the good news of your love,
that all who hear it
may be reconciled to you;
through him who died for us and rose again
and reigns with you and the Holy Spirit,
one God, now and for ever. *JLG (adapted)*

Easter Eve

Grant, Lord,
that we who are baptized into the death
of your Son our Saviour Jesus Christ
may continually put to death our evil desires
and be buried with him;
that through the grave and gate of death
we may pass to our joyful resurrection,
through his merits, who died and was buried
and rose again for us,
your son Jesus Christ our Lord.
1928 Prayer Book (adapted)

Easter Day

Lord of all life and power,
through the mighty resurrection of your Son
you have overcome the old order of sin and death
and have made all things new in him.
Grant that we, being dead to sin
and alive to you in Jesus Christ,
may reign with him in glory;
to whom with you and the Holy Spirit
be praise and honour, glory and might,
now and in all eternity.

JLG

Easter 1

1   Almighty Father,
who in your great mercy made glad the disciples
    with the sight of the risen Lord:
give us such knowledge of his presence with us,
that we may be strengthened and sustained by his
    risen life
and serve you continually in righteousness and truth;
through Jesus Christ our Lord.

JLG

2   Almighty God,
you have given us the true bread from heaven,
Jesus Christ your Son.
Grant that we may be fed by him
    who gives life to the world,
    that we may abide in him and he in us;
        who lives and reigns with you and the Holy
            Spirit,
        one God, now and forever.
            Macnutt, The Prayer Manual, 398 (adapted)

Easter 2

1   God of peace,
who brought again from the dead
    our Lord Jesus Christ,
that great shepherd of the sheep,
by the blood of the eternal covenant:
make us perfect in every good work
    to do your will,
and work in us that which is well-pleasing
    in your sight;
through Jesus Christ our Lord.
*   JLG (adaptation of Hebrews 13:20)*

2   Lord Jesus Christ, the shepherd of your people,
    protect us by your care
    and strengthen us by your risen presence:
    that when we hear your voice
        calling us each by name,
        we may follow wherever you are leading,
        for your Name's sake.

Easter 3

Almighty God,
whose Son Jesus Christ is the resurrection and the life
    of all who put their trust in him:
raise us, we pray, from the death of sin
    to the life of righteousness;
that we may seek the things which are above,
where he reigns with you and the Holy Spirit,
one God, now and for ever.
*   Anglican Series 2, Burial Service (adapted)*

Easter 4

1   Almighty God,
        who alone can bring order
        to the unruly wills and passions of sinful people:
        give us grace,
             to love what you command
             and to desire what you promise,
        that in all the changes and chances of this world,
        our hearts may surely there be fixed
        where lasting joys are to be found;
        through Jesus Christ our Lord.   *BCP (adapted)*

2   Almighty God,
             whom to know is everlasting life:
             grant us so truly to know your Son Jesus Christ
             to be the way, the truth, and the life,
             that we may steadfastly follow him
                  in the way that leads to life eternal;
                  through the same Jesus Christ your Son our
                       Lord.
                            BCP, St Philip and St James (adapted)

Easter 5

1   Almighty and everlasting God,
        you are always more ready to hear than we to pray
        and give more than either we desire or deserve.
        Pour down upon us the abundance of your mercy,
             forgiving us those things of which our conscience is
                  afraid
        and giving us those good things which we are not
                  worthy to ask
             save through the merits and mediation
                  of Jesus Christ your Son our Lord.
                            BCP, Trinity 12 (adapted)

2   Eternal Father,
        whose Son Jesus Christ ascended to the throne
                of heaven
        that he might rule over all things as Lord:
        keep the Church in the unity of the Spirit
        and in the bond of his peace,
        and bring the whole created order
                to worship at his feet,
        who is alive and reigns with you and the Holy Spirit,
        one God, now and for ever.   *JLG*

Ascension Day

Almighty God,
as we believe your only-begotten Son, our Lord
        Jesus Christ has ascended into the heavens,
so may we also in heart and mind thither ascend
and with him continually dwell;
who is alive and reigns with you and the Holy Spirit,
one God, now and for ever.

                            BCP (adapted)

Easter 6

Eternal Father,
whose Son Jesus Christ, when he returned to glory,
did not leave us comfortless
but sent the Holy Spirit to remain with us for ever:
grant that the same Spirit may bring us
        at last to that heavenly home,
where Christ has gone before to prepare a place,
and where with you and the Holy Spirit
he is worshipped and glorified, now and for ever.
                    BCP, Sunday after Ascension (adapted)

Pentecost

1   Almighty God,
       who at this time
       taught the hearts of your faithful people
       by sending to them the light of your Holy Spirit:
       grant us by the same Spirit
              to have a right judgement in all things,
       and evermore to rejoice in his holy comfort;
       through the merits of Christ Jesus our Saviour,
       who is alive and reigns with you
              in the unity of the Spirit,
       one God, now and for ever.   *BCP (adapted)*

2   Almighty God,
       who sent your Holy Spirit to the disciples
       with the wind from heaven and in tongues of flame,
       filling them with joy
              and boldness to preach the gospel:
       send us out in the power of the same Spirit
       to witness to your truth
       and to draw all men to the fire of your love;
       through Jesus Christ our Lord.   *JLG*

Pentecost 1 (Trinity Sunday)

1   Almighty and everlasting God,
       you have given us your servants grace,
       by the confession of a true faith
              to acknowledge the glory of the eternal trinity,
       and in the power of the divine majesty
              to worship the unity.
       Keep us steadfast in this faith,
       that we may evermore be defended from all adversities,

through Jesus Christ our Lord
who is alive and reigns with you and the Holy Spirit,
one God, now and for ever.

Alternative Services, Series 3, Collects

2   Almighty and eternal God,
you have revealed yourself as Father, Son,
    and Holy Spirit,
and live and reign in the perfect unity of love.
Keep us steadfast in this faith,
that we may know you in all your ways
and evermore rejoice in your eternal glory.
who are three persons in one God,
now and for ever.

CSI, Pentecost 1 (adapted)

Pentecost 2

Almighty and everlasting God,
by whose Spirit the whole body of your faithful people
    is governed and sanctified:
hear our prayer which we offer for all members
    of your Holy Church:
that each in his vocation and ministry
may serve you in holiness and truth
to the glory of your name;
through our Lord and Saviour Jesus Christ.

BCP (adapted)

Pentecost 3

Lord God our Father,
through our Saviour Jesus Christ
you have assured all people of eternal life

and in baptism have made us one with him.
Deliver us from the death of sin
and raise us to new life in your love,
by the grace of our Lord Jesus Christ,
in the fellowship of the Holy Spirit.

JLG

Pentecost 4

Almighty God,
you have broken the tyranny of sin
and have sent the Spirit of your Son into our hearts
whereby we call you Father.
Give us grace to dedicate our freedom to your service
that all people may be brought
to the glorious liberty of the children of God;
through Jesus Christ our Lord.

JLG (adapted)

Pentecost 5

Almighty God,
you show to those who are in error
the light of your truth,
that they may return to the way of righteousness.
May we and all who have been admitted
to the fellowship of Christ's religion
reject those things which are contrary to our profession
and follow all such things as are agreeable to the same;
through Jesus Christ our Lord.

BCP, Easter 3 (adapted)

Pentecost 6

O God,
since without you
we are not able to please you:
mercifully grant that your Holy Spirit
may in all things direct and rule our hearts;
through Jesus Christ our Lord.

BCP, Trinity 19 (adapted)

Pentecost 7

Lord, you have taught us
that all our doings without love
    are nothing worth.
Send your Holy Spirit
and pour into our hearts
    that most excellent gift of love,
the true bond of peace and of all virtues,
without which whoever lives is counted dead before you.
Grant this for the sake of your only Son,
Jesus Christ our Lord.

BCP, Quinquagesima (adapted)

Pentecost 8

Almighty God,
    you sent your Spirit
    to abide in your Church unto the end.
May we receive the gifts of his grace
    and bring forth the fruit of the Spirit;
    through Jesus Christ our Lord.

Scottish Prayer Book,
Whitsun Postcommunion Collect (adapted)

Pentecost 9

Almighty God,
you see that we have no power of ourselves
    to help ourselves.
Keep us both outwardly in our bodies
    and inwardly in our souls,
that we may be defended from all adversities
    which may happen to the body,
and from all evil thoughts
    which may assault and hurt the soul;
through Jesus Christ our Lord.   *BCP, Lent 2 (adapted)*

Pentecost 10

Father of all,
who gave your only-begotten Son
to take upon himself the form of a servant
and to be obedient even to death on a cross:
give us the same mind that was in Christ Jesus
that, sharing his humility,
we may come to be with him in his glory;
who is alive and reigns with you and the Holy Spirit,
one God, now and for ever.   *JLG (adapted)*

Pentecost 11

Almighty Father,
whose Son Jesus Christ has taught us
that what we do for the least of our brethren
    we do also for him:
give us the will to be the servant of others
    as he was the servant of all,
who gave up his life and died for us,
but is alive and reigns with you and the Holy Spirit,
one God, now and for ever.

St Augustine (adapted)

Pentecost 12

Almighty God,
who called your Church to witness
that you were in Christ
    reconciling the world to yourself:
help us to proclaim the good news of your love,
that all who hear it
    may be reconciled to you;
through him who died for us and rose again
and reigns with you and the Holy Spirit,
one God, now and for ever.

JLG (adapted)

Pentecost 13

Lord God,
whose blessed Son our Saviour
gave his back to the smiters
and did not hide his face from shame:
give us grace to endure the sufferings
    of this present time
with sure confidence in the glory that shall be revealed;
through Jesus Christ our Lord.

American Prayer Book,
Tuesday before Easter (adapted)

Pentecost 14

Almighty God,
you have taught us through your Son
that love is the fulfilling of the law.
Grant that we may love you with our whole heart
and our neighbours as ourselves;
through Jesus Christ our Lord.

Pentecost 15

Lord God,
the protector of all who trust in you,
without whom nothing is strong,
     nothing is holy:
increase and multiply upon us your mercy,
that you being our ruler and guide,
we may so pass through things temporal
that we finally lose not the things eternal.
Grant this, heavenly Father,
for the sake of Jesus Christ our Lord.

BCP, Trinity 4 (adapted)

Pentecost 16

Almighty Father,
whose will is to restore all things
     in your beloved Son, the king of all:
govern the hearts and minds of those in authority,
and bring the families of the nations,
divided and torn apart by the ravages of sin,
to be subject to his most gentle rule;
who is alive and reigns with you and the Holy Spirit,
one God, now and for ever.

JLG

Pentecost 17

Lord of all power and might,
the author and giver of all good things:
graft in our hearts the love of your name,
increase in us true religion,
nourish in us all goodness,
and of your great mercy keep us in the same;
through Jesus Christ our Lord.

BCP, Trinity 7 (adapted)

Pentecost 18

Almighty God,
you have made us for yourself,
and our souls are restless
till they find their rest in you.
Teach us to offer ourselves to your service,
that here we may have your peace,
and in the world to come may see you face to face;
through Jesus Christ our Lord.

JLG

Pentecost 19

Almighty and everliving God,
increase in us your gift of faith;
that, forsaking what lies behind
and reaching out to that which is before us,
we may run the way of your commandments
and win the crown of everlasting joy;
through Jesus Christ our Lord.

Anglican Series 3, Collects

Pentecost 20

Merciful God,
you have prepared for those who love you
such good things as pass human understanding.
Pour into our hearts such love towards you
that we, loving you above all things,
may obtain your promises,
which exceed all that we can desire;
through Jesus Christ our Lord.

BCP, Trinity 6 (adapted)

Pentecost 21
Almighty God,
your Son has opened for us
a new and living way into your presence.
Give us pure hearts and steadfast wills
to worship you in spirit and in truth;
through Jesus Christ our Lord.

JLG

EXTRA SUNDAYS AFTER PENTECOST

1 Stir up, O Lord,
   the wills of your faithful people;
   that richly bearing the fruit of good works,
   they may by you be richly rewarded;
   through Jesus Christ our Lord.

   BCP, Trinity 25 (adapted)

2 Heavenly Father,
   whose blessed Son was revealed
            that he might destroy the works of the devil
   and make us the children of God
   and heirs of eternal life:
   grant that we, having this hope,
   may purify ourselves even as he is pure;
   that when he shall appear in power and great glory
   we may be made like him in his eternal and
            glorious kingdom;
   where he is alive and reigns with you and
            the Holy Spirit,
   one God, now and for ever.

   BCP, Epiphany 6 (adapted)

COLLECTS FOR SPECIAL DAYS

Christian Unity

1   O God, Creator and Father of all,
      by your Holy Spirit you have made
      a diversity of peoples one
        in the confession of your name.
    Lead them, by the same Spirit,
      to show to the whole earth
      one mind in belief
      and one passion for righteousness;
        through Jesus Christ our Lord.

CSI (adapted)

2   Father, Son, and Holy Spirit,
    holy and undivided Trinity,
    three persons in one God:
      inspire your whole Church,
      founded upon this faith,
      to witness under many forms
      to the perfect unity of your love,
        one God, now and for ever.
Alternative Services, Series 3, Collects, Unity 2

Springtime

1   Almighty God, Lord of heaven and earth,
    pour out your blessing upon this land,
      and give us a fruitful season.
    Grant that we, who constantly receive your bounty,
      may evermore give thanks in your holy Church;
        through Jesus Christ our Lord.
American Prayer Book, Collect for Rogation Days

2   Almighty God,
            whose will it is
            that the earth should bear its fruits in their seasons:

            direct the labours of those who work on the land,
            that they may employ the resources of nature
            to your glory for our own well-being,
            and the relief of those in need;
            through Jesus Christ our Lord.
      Alternative Services, Series 3, Collects, Rogation (3)

Harvest Festival

Almighty God,
      we offer you hearty thanks
      for your fatherly goodness and care
      in giving to us the fruits of the earth
            in their season.
Grant us grace
      to use them to your glory,
      for the relief of those in need,
      and our own well-being;
through Jesus Christ, the living Bread
      who came down from heaven
      and gives life to the world
      and who lives and reigns with you,
            the Father and the Holy Spirit,
            one God, now and ever.   *CSI (adapted)*

Michaelmas

Eternal Lord God,
            you have appointed both angels and people
            to worship and serve you in your kingdom.

As your holy angels stand before you in heaven,
    so may they help and defend us here on earth;
    through Jesus Christ our Lord.

Alternative Services, Series 3, Collects

Overseas

1   O God, our heavenly Father,
        you showed your love
        by sending your only Son into the world
        that all might live through him.
    Pour your Spirit upon your Church,
        that she may fulfil his command
        to make disciples of all nations.
    Send forth labourers into your harvest,
        and hasten the time
        when all shall be gathered in and saved;
        through Jesus Christ our Lord.

Scottish BCP (adapted)

2   Lord,
        you have consecrated our world
        by sending your Son into the midst of it
        and by making all things new in him.
    Give us and all your people,
        the courage and power we need
        to share fully in his mission to the world
        and to further his kingdom in the lives of all.

New Every Morning, 1973 (very slightly altered)

All Saints

Almighty God,
>you have knit together your elect
>in one communion and fellowship
>in the mystical body of your Son.

Give us grace to follow your blessed saints
>in all virtuous and godly living,
>that we may come to those unspeakable joys
>which you have prepared
>for those who perfectly love you;
>through Jesus Christ our Lord.

Alternative Services, Series 3, Collects

Remembrance Day

1   Lord God,
>>keep us mindful of all your benefits
>>and heedful of our high calling,
>>that we may yield ourselves
>>in new obedience to your holy will,
>>and live henceforth as those who are not their own,
>>but are bought with a price;
>>through Jesus Christ our Lord.

>*BCO—Remembrance Sunday Service (adapted)*

2   O God,
>>by whose wisdom and power
>>the wrath of humankind is turned to your praise:
>>overrule our passions and designs,
>>and grant, for the sake of those whose lives were
>>>lost in war,
>>and for the sake of the generations to come,
>>that the nations of the world may learn your ways

and your kingdom of peace may prevail on earth;
through Jesus Christ our Lord.

New Every Morning, 1973 (adapted)

St Andrew's Day

Almighty God,

who gave such grace to your apostle Saint Andrew
that he readily obeyed the calling of your Son
and brought his brother with him:

give us, who are called by your holy word,

grace to follow without delay
and to tell the good news of your kingdom;
through Jesus Christ our Lord.

Alternative Services, Series 3, Collects, Rogation (3)

Resource Bibliography

BOOKS OF COMPLETE SERVICES with prayers which are immediately usable

1   *Prayers For Sunday Services*, The Saint Andrew Press, 1980.
2   *Prayers For Contemporary Worship*, The Saint Andrew Press, 1977.
3   *Worship Now*, The Saint Andrew Press, 1972.
4   *Companion to The Lectionary; Volume 3, A New Collection of Prayers,* Neil Dixon, Epworth Press, 1983.
5   *Companion to the Lectionary; Volume 4, Prayers of Intercession,* Christine Odell, Epworth Press, 1987.
6   *New Prayers for Worship*, Alan Gaunt, John Paul The Preacher's Press, 1972.
7   *Prayers for the Christian Year*, Alan Gaunt, John Paul The Preacher's Press, 1980.
8   *People Praying,* Ian Cowie, The Saint Andrew Press, 1972.
9   *The Worship Book, Services,* The Westminster/John Knox Press, Kentucky, 1975.
10 *A Wee Worship Book*, Wild Goose Publications, 1987.
11 *The Book of Alternative Services of the Anglican Church of Canada,* Anglican Book Centre, Toronto, 1985.

BOOKS OF PRAYERS from which selection would required to be made.

1   *Praying Together in Word and Song*, Taizé, Mowbray, revised, 1985.

2 *New Every Morning*, BBC, 1973.
3 *Contemporary Prayers for Public Worship*, edited by Caryl Micklem, SCM Press, 1967.
4 *More Contemporary Prayers for Public Worship*, edited by Caryl Micklem, SCM Press, 1970.
5 *Contemporary Prayers for Church and School,* edited by Caryl Micklem, SCM Press, 1975.
6 *Prayers for all Seasons*, Beryl Bye, Lutterworth Press, Cambridge, first published 1971, reprinted edition 1987.
7 *The Hodder Book of Christian Prayers,* Tony Castle, Hodder & Stoughton, London, 1986.
8 *Prayers for the Church Community,* Roy Chapman and Donald Hilton, National Christian Education Council, 1978.
9 *Parish Prayers,* Frank Colquhoun, first published 1967, twelfth impression, Hodder & Stoughton, 1987.
10 *Contemporary Parish Prayers,* Frank Colquhoun, Hodder & Stoughton, 1975.
11 *New Parish Prayers,* Frank Colquhoun, Hodder & Stoughton, 1982.
12 *A Healing House of Prayer*, Morris Maddocks, Hodder & Stoughton, 1987.
13 *More Prayers for Today's Church,* edited by R H L Williams, Kingsway Publications, 1984.
14 *A Diary of Reading,* John Baillie, first edition 1955, first paperback edition, Oxford University Press, 1981.
15 *Prayers and Praises*, Nathaniel Micklem, The Saint Andrew Press, 1982 edition.
16 *The Oxford Book of Prayer*, edited by G Appleton, Oxford University Press, 1988.
17 *New Ways to Worship*, Committee on Public Worship and Aids to Devotion, The Saint Andrew Press, 1980.
18 *The Daily Office Revised, with other Prayers and Services,* R C D Jasper, SPCK, 1978.

19 *Prayers written at Vailima*, R L Stevenson, Chatto & Windus, 1916.
20 *Kyrie Eleison,* H J Wotherspoon, Blackwood, Edinburgh 1899.
21 *The Whole Earth Shall Cry Glory*, Macleod, Wild Goose Publications, 1985.
22 *Iona Community Worship Book,* Wild Goose Publications, 1988.
23 *Your Will Be Done (Prayers and Readings),* Christian Conference of Asia.
24 *A Worship Book (Vancouver),*World Council of Churches Geneva, 1984.
25 The New Moon of the Seasons, *Prayers from Carmina Gadelica,* Floris Books, 1986.
26 Sun Dances, *Prayers from Carmina Gadelica*, Floris Books, 1985.
27 *Work in Worship*, Norman Goodacre, Mowbrays, 1980.
29 *A Kind of Praying,* Rex Chapman, SCM, 1976.

BOOKS OF QUARRY MATERIALS in which ideas for both form and content of a Service could be found.

1 *Words for Worship*, edited by Christopher Campling and Michael Davis, Edward Arnold, 1969.
2 *Daily Prayers*, edited by Eric Milner White and G W Briggs, Pelican, 1959 (or later editions).
3 *Prayers of Life*, Michael Quoist, Gill & MacMillan, 1966.
4 *No Longer Strangers,* World Council of Churches, 1983.
5 *Celebrating One World* (A resource book on Liturgy and Social Justice), CAFOD.
6 *At all Times and in all Places*, Myra Blyth and Tony Jasper, Marshall Pickering, 1986.
7 *Pocket Praise*, Stainer and Bell, 1980.

BOOKS with material and suggestions suitable for reading and meditation at a Service.

1   *A Word in Season,* compiled by Donald Hilton (NCEC), 1984.
2   *Short Prayers for the Long Day,* Harcourt, Giles & Melville, Collins Liturgical Publications, London, 1978.
3   *A Private Devotional Diary,* edited by John Birkbeck, The Drummond Press, 1977.
4   *The Prayers of the New Testament,* D Coggan, Hodder & Stoughton, London, 1967.
5   *"Tell Them To Me", Parables in contemporary settings,* Gwyn Filby, Elmvest, 1986.
6   *Sermons for the Christian Year,* John Paul The Preacher's Press.
7   *The Words of Christ, Forty Meditations,* Frank Topping, Lutterworth Press, 1983.
    Also in the same series:
    Lord of Time, 1985.
    Lord of the Evening, 1979.
    Lord of the Morning, 1977.
    Lord of Life, 1982.
    Lord of my Days, 1980.
    Lord of the Seasons (by Peter Firth), 1978.
8   *Readings for the Senior Assembly,* and *More Readings for the Assembly,* D M Prescott, Blandford Press, 1973.
9   *More Words for Worship,* Michael Davis, Arnold, 1975.
10 *Readings,* Denys Thomson, Cambridge University Press, 1979.
11 *Worship and Wonder,* E S P Jones, Galliard Ltd, 1971.
12 *News Extra,* Edward Banyard, Galliard Ltd, 1971.
13 *Words Alive,* Edward Banyard, Belton Books, 1969.
14 *Reflections on the Gospels,* J M Talbot, Word Books, 1987.
15 *All Year Round,* BBC, annually.

16 *Imagining the Gospels,* K Galloway, SPCK, 1988.
17 *Preaching Through the Christian Year,* Frank Colquhoun,
    Mowbray.
18 *Wild Goose Prints 1, 2, 3* (Drama for Worship), Wild
    Goose Publications, 1985, 1986, 1987.
19 *Eh . . . Jesus . . . , Yes Peter?* (Dialogues for Worship),
    Wild Goose Publications, 1987.
20 *Act Justly* (Drama for Worship), Christian Aid/CAFOD
21 *Expository Times,* T&T Clark, monthly.

Notes

Notes

Notes

Notes

Notes

Notes

Notes

Notes

Notes

Notes

Notes

Notes

Notes